CALAMITY JANE

CALAMITY JANE

A STUDY IN HISTORICAL CRITICISM

by

ROBERTA BEED SOLLID

A.A., Stephens College, 1936
B.A., Stanford University, 1938
M.A., Montana State University, 1951

Correlated and edited by Vivian A. Paladin
Indexed by John Hakola
With new Foreword by Vivian A. Paladin,
Introduction by James D. McLaird, and
Afterword by Richard W. Etulain.

Montana Historical Society Press, Helena

Front cover art by William George from "Calamity Jane," *Argosy*, May 1958, p. 31.

Back cover: Photograph of Calamity Jane by C. E. Finn, Livingston, Montana, probably in the mid-1890s. (Montana Historical Society Photograph Archives)

Cover design by Finstad Visual Design, Helena, Montana

Pages 1 through 147 are reproduced from the original edition of *Calamity Jane* published by the Montana Historical Society (Western Press) in 1958. The preceeding materials, original and new, and the new afterword were typeset in New Century Schoolbook for the 1995 edition.

Printed by Thomson-Shore, Inc., Dexter, Michigan

Library of Congress Cataloging-in-Publication Data

Sollid, Roberta Beed, 1916–

  Calamity Jane : a study in historical criticism / by Roberta Beed Sollid ; correlated and edited by Vivian A. Paladin ; indexed by John Hakola ; with a new foreword by Vivian A. Paladin ; introduction by James D. McLaird ; and afterword by Richard W. Etulain.

     p. cm.

  Originally published: [Helena] : Western Press, c1958.

  Includes bibliographical references (p.) and index.

  ISBN 0-917298-33-0 : $14.95

  1. Calamity Jane, 1852–1903. 2. Pioneers—West (U.S.)—Biography. 3. West (U.S.)—Biography. I. Title.

F594.C2S6 1995 94–48732

978'.02'092—dc20 CIP

ABOUT THE AUTHOR

Mrs. Roberta Beed Sollid, whose scholarly manuscript on the life of Calamity Jane is published in this book, is a "transplanted" Westerner. Born in Hampton, Iowa, in 1916, she lived in Streator, Ill., as a child. She attended Stephens College in Columbia, Mo., and took her A.A. Degree there in 1936.

California became more or less her permanent home when she went to Palo Alto to take her B.A. Degree from Stanford in 1938. She received a California teaching certificate from the State College in San Francisco in 1940, and she taught school and did office work until 1942, when she became a communications officer in the U. S. Navy.

She married Kjell Sollid, a native of Norway, in 1943, and they have a daughter, Inge, born in 1945. Mrs. Sollid and her family moved to Missoula in 1947, and it was then that she began a study of Montana and Northwest history "more or less in self defense."

Mrs. Sollid recalls: "My new friends spoke an entirely different language than I did. They knew so much of their local history that I decided to enroll in Dr. Paul Phillips' history class. He was instrumental in getting me to continue with my graduate work. I more or less forgot my friends and began work in the "stacks."

Thus the research into the life of one of the West's most colorful and enigmatic women began.

The Sollids returned to California after Mrs. Sollid received her M.A. Degree in History from Montana State University [now the University of Montana, Missoula] in 1951. They live in San Diego, where the author's husband is an insurance man. Mrs. Sollid says her absorbing interests now are her home and family and teaching beginners in the modern dance at State College.

1994 note: Roberta Beed Sollid still lives in San Diego, California.

NOTE FROM THE PUBLISHER [1958]

This book, the second in a series of restricted editions published by the Western Press of the Historical Society of Montana, is a critical study into the life of Calamity Jane.

The Western Press believes this manuscript worthy of publication because it is a truly scholarly effort to set the record straight concerning Calamity Jane. It is not sensational writing—scholarly writing rarely is. But we think it will be read with interest by those who regard the facts of history as more fascinating than the myths.

The Western Press is indebted to many people for their help in collecting pictures of Calamity Jane and of some of the people who figured in the history of the period during which she lived. Much help was also received in attemping to date the pictures of Calamity Jane, and to tell the circumstances under which they were taken, and by whom.

Where we found a little story connected with the pictures, we placed that information in the Picture Notes Section at the back of the book. There may be some whimsy in these recollections, but we do not believe they will detract from the historical accuracy of the text.

The publishers wish to thank the following persons for their assistance in gathering the pictures used in this book, and in many cases for information regarding them:

Miss Virginia Walton, Librarian, Historical Society of Montana; J. Leonard Jennewein, Dakota Wesleyan University, Mitchell, S.D.; Will G. Robinson, Secretary, South Dakota State Historical Society, Pierre, S. D.; Mrs. Ruth Huffman Scott of The Huffman Studios, Miles City, Mont.; Mrs. Alys Freeze, Western History Department, Public Library, Denver, Colo.; Gene M. Gressley, Archivist, University of Wyoming, Laramie, Wyo.; A. R. McMicken, Rawlins, Wyo.; and Mrs. Agnes Wright Spring, Historian, State Historical Society of Colorado.

THE PUBLISHERS

TABLE OF CONTENTS

LIST OF ILLUSTRATIONS

LIST OF ILLUSTRATIONS (*continued*)

Photographer C. E. Finn took this photograph of Calamity Jane in Livingston, Montana, probably in the mid-1890s. (Montana Historical Society Photograph Archives)

CALAMITY JANE
Foreword by Vivian A. Paladin

It was in the summer of 1957 that I got to know a notoriously loose woman named Calamity Jane and a treasured repository of information about our past named the Montana Historical Society. My acquaintance with the former lasted only long enough to see to book publication a carefully researched study of her strange and checkered life written in 1951 as a master's thesis at the University of Montana (then Montana State University) by Roberta Beed Sollid. My acquaintance with the historical society blossomed into a career that was to span over two decades and develop into a personal and professional love affair that persists to this day.

Dr. K. Ross Toole, then director of the Montana Historical Society, had known about me and my roots in journalism but our paths had not crossed since we were both students at the University of Montana many years before. Renewing a friendship with him and his family, he perceived I might be at loose ends in a strange city (I had moved to Helena with my family in 1956). He told me about a thesis on Calamity Jane that had languished in the files for several years but which he believed had such unusual merit that it deserved publication as one of a series of limited edition books he envisioned for the historical society. Short of editorial help, he suggested I take on the task of editing and correlating.

I recall I protested quite vigorously that my experience had all been in newspaper journalism, although I confessed that I had long harbored a wish to write about historical subjects. "Just give it a try, Viv," Ross said with typical you-can-do-it confidence. And so I set to work, spending a lot of my time gathering pictures of the mannish-looking Calamity, striving for accuracy in writing captions and appendix notes about them, and in organizing the manuscript into book form. I recall vividly the decision to make the dust jacket a vivid red, suggestive of the notorious subject, and the agonizing decision to publish a picture of her in virginal white as she lay in her coffin in Deadwood, South Dakota.

I must confess now that I did not realize at the time just how good the manuscript was and how enduring Roberta Sollid's research and writing would prove to be. I lacked the experience to recognize the value of serious archival research and on-the-scene investigation into a subject such as this. For in truth, while the life and the real or fictional activities of Calamity Jane are still not the stuff of great history, she lived at a time of historical importance. Perhaps what is even more important, she represents a regrettable trend beginning in the 1920s to glorify and glamorize notorious western figures. Pulp writers, sensation seekers, and even Hollywood producers all contributed to creating and perpetuating all manner of myths and downright lies about them. The rough, hard-drinking, profane Calamity Jane became a glamour queen, a "Joan of Arc" of the frontier, the romance in the lives of military officers and such frontier characters as Buffalo Bill Cody and Wild Bill Hickok. Roberta Sollid came as close as anyone had ever come to getting at the truth about Calamity Jane, debunking much of the incredible distortions of others. Serious historians today have long credited this modest little book, copies of which are scarce today, with being for many years the most reliable source study of this strange woman.

Thus it was that I undertook a task more important than I knew. Usually, whenever I saw a copy of the book, I thought about how certain things could or should have been done differently, perhaps more professionally. But mostly I gave it credit for "getting my foot in the door" at the historical society.

I recall admiring Roberta Sollid for her persistent research, but until recently, when we renewed a from-afar acquaintance by telephone and the mails, I did not realize just how persistent she had been back in 1948 when she was a graduate student under the late Professor Paul Phillips of the university's history department in Missoula.

She told me about an orientation session during which she and other students of Dr. Phillips were considering subjects for research and writing. The name Calamity Jane came up, and Roberta said she immediately asked if a person called by that bizarre name had ever lived. Dr. Phillips assured her that indeed there had been such a person, that she had spent some time in Montana, but that so much fiction and exaggerated stories had been told, written, and portrayed about her that no one knew what the real facts were. Indeed, few if any had ever really tried to find out.

Noting that this new graduate student, who was from the Midwest, held a B.A. from Stephens College in Missouri and an A.B. in psychology from Stanford, Professor Phillips wanted to know why she had asked the question about Calamity Jane. Roberta explained to him, as she did to me, that when she was a little girl and taking dancing lessons, she also liked to play hard with the other children in her neighborhood and was constantly skinning her knees. It invariably happened around recital time, she said, much to the distress of her mother.

"She began calling me Calamity Jane every time this happened," Roberta recalled, "but of course neither of us had the remotest idea of who Calamity Jane might be. It was a name Mother had heard somewhere, and the Calamity part seemed to fit the predicaments my scabby knees were continually getting me into."

It did not take much persuading on the part of Dr. Phillips to convince Roberta Sollid that the real Calamity Jane deserved careful research and was a unique and worthy topic for her master's thesis. Dr. Phillips's own extensive library offered a good place to start, but after his untimely death an over-zealous custodian made it virtually impossible to use those resources. The result was that Roberta Sollid began spending weekends at the Montana Historical Society in Helena, aided during off hours by dedicated and cooperative librarians. She also made visits to towns Calamity Jane was known to have lived in or visited briefly, searching through newspapers and other archival material. Her searches took her to historical societies, libraries, and newspaper offices in Montana, Colorado, Wyoming, Nebraska, Minnesota, South Dakota, and even Chicago. It was in the contemporary press that even short news items showed up that placed Calamity at a certain place at a certain time, sometimes refuting Calamity's own claims or those of others.

Finally, Roberta decided she had to get to Deadwood, the place most identified with Calamity Jane in life and in death. Traveling by bus, she interviewed as many people as possible en route but really struck pay dirt in Deadwood, where she found the people generally friendly and cooperative. Those still living shared reminiscences, and newspaper publishers and writers usually told her what they knew or showed her their writings. Staying at the historic Franklin Hotel in Deadwood, which was operating in the days of Calamity Jane, Roberta met a number of people who remembered her, although at least one man regretted he had not gone to her funeral because he had not realized she would someday be better known than she was in 1903.

One of the most interesting places she visited in Deadwood, and she visited there more than once, was Mt. Moriah Cemetery where Calamity Jane is buried. Roberta encountered many people there, some of them tourists who had, like her, not known there really had been a woman named Calamity Jane. Stories were told that Calamity had made a dying wish that she be buried next to Wild Bill Hickok, who had been shot to death in a Deadwood saloon in 1876. Her wishes were carried out, although some of her own claims about disarming Hickok's killer and indeed the truth about her relationship with the famed frontiersman are as elusive as many other "facts" about her life.

Almost all those Sollid interviewed agreed that Calamity Jane had compassion for the underdog, for the ill and down-at-the-heels, but all womanly goodness and tenderness disappeared when she became increasingly lost in sodden alcoholism. As one of her acquaintances put it, "Lots of us . . . knew the better side of Calamity; but then, you know, she would go to these bawdy houses and dance halls and it was whoopee and soon she was drunk and then, well, things just sort of went haywire with old Calamity."

It is a validation of the work of Roberta Sollid and a salute to the foresight of Dr. Toole that the historical society republishes this manuscript after so many years. For me, it was a momentous step into the realm of historical publication when I was asked to participate the first time around. Today, it is a special treat to be asked to reminisce about it the second time around. One might even be tempted to raise an innocent and pious glass to old Calamity.

Martha Jane Canary, popularly known as Calamity Jane, probably posed for this portrait in Pierre, South Dakota, circa 1901. (Montana Historical Society Photograph Archives)

PREFACE [1958]

No career is so elusive to the historian as that of a loose woman. Calamity Jane was that sort of woman, and known details about her life are hard to find. Like most prostitutes and drunkards she left little behind in the way of tangible evidence which could be used by historians to reconstruct the story of her checkered career.

During her many years of cavorting about the frontier, Calamity Jane gained notoriety and a certain amount of fame as a character, enough at least so that the newspapers mentioned her when she was in town. She caused so much commotion that she could scarcely be overlooked. Her real ascent to fame, however, began some twenty years after her death in 1903 and after the death of those who knew her best. She was all but forgotten by her contemporaries until, for some unknown reason, sensation-writers and historians began to take an interest in her. Incidents and stories of her almost forgotten life then became popular. As the vogue for Calamity Jane stories increased, prodigious quantities of material containing a paucity of truth were written about her. She became the heroine of many a tale that found ready sale during the 1920's and 1930's. If facts were not known, they were invented. No one could prove them false.[1]

This study of Calamity Jane will attempt to ascertain the facts of her career, so far as they can be determined, and to evaluate the various accounts left by her many chroniclers. The account should separate the folklore and legend

---

[1] Recently the motion-picture industry has capitalized on this woman's career. Among numerous Hollywood films depicting western life and characters, these five will serve to illustrate the place that Calamity Jane has attained (Note the glamorous actresses who portrayed the plainswoman): *The Plainsman* (Jean Arthur); *Wild Bill Hickok*; *The Paleface* (Jane Russell); *Calamity Jane and Sam Bass* (Yvonne de Carlo); *Texan Meets Calamity Jane.*

of her life from established facts.[2] The latter should reveal her true character. Much new material has been gathered which will fill in the gaps in the life of this woman and clear up many points previously disregarded or badly distorted.

Material was gathered for this study in the summer of 1949 on an extended trip into country once roamed by Calamity Jane. This included numerous towns in Montana, South Dakota and Wyoming. Individuals ranging from Catholic nuns to a Deadwood bar-tender who was a pallbearer at Jane's funeral were consulted for details of her life. Of the fifty people interviewed, about ten can be credited with dependable contributions. More valuable were old newspaper files found in publishing offices and libraries.[3] While newspaper articles may be short-lived, they often give a more accurate picture of day-to-day thoughts, feelings and reactions of people to events than do many scholarly works. Mention of Calamity Jane in any newspaper is important to this study because it establishes her whereabouts on or near a particular date. Enough of these dates indicate a pattern or trend which may be used to determine the truth of her own stories or those repeated by other people.

Other sources were hard to find. County records were of little value because they often were not kept until too late a date to be of much help. For example, an attempt to start an orderly system of recording did not begin in Montana until the territory became a state in 1889. No personal letters to, from or about Calamity Jane were found, and only

---

[2] Three students worked recently on studies of Calamity Jane: Clarence Paine, librarian, writer of numerous historical articles, and instructor in history at Beloit College, has prepared a study of Calamity Jane; Dr. Nolie Mumey, physician and writer of historical articles, in 1950 published his book, *Calamity Jane*; and Marie M. Augspurger, author of *Yellowstone Park*, has worked on a volume entitled *The West's Joan of Arc*.

[3] Newspaper offices and city libraries proved to be of much less value than state historical collections. The two former agencies have in many cases turned over their entire files to the latter, thus making much research material available in one place. The following historical libraries were used: Montana Historical Library, South Dakota Historical Library, Wyoming Historical Library, Minnesota Historical Library, and Chicago Historical Library.

two relevant diaries discovered, each of which contained only one sentence about her. The majority of people who wrote letters or kept diaries were not concerned with women of Calamity Jane's type. Consequently, with the exception of newspaper notices, her name did not appear frequently in contemporary records. Many years later, however, after she had been glamorized as a type of western "wild woman," people who had once known her began to write of her in their recollections and memoirs. While earlier they had thought her insignificant, they later became conscious of her importance, or at least of society's interest in her.

Present-day opinion about Calamity Jane varies from the frequently-met belief that no such person existed to the complete acceptance of all the fantastic stories about her. At the grave of Calamity Jane the author heard both views expressed. Many tourists seemed surprised when they saw the tomb marker at Mt. Moriah Cemetery in Deadwood and exclaimed that they did not know she was a real person. Their local guides, probably their relatives or friends, sensed an opportunity to expound on local history, and credited Calamity Jane with doing and saying things which she, herself, probably would not have thought of even in her wildest dreams.

People of the older generation in Deadwood were not pleased to know that further research was being made on such a person as Calamity Jane. They thought her of no consequence and not at all important in Deadwood history. They expressed surprise that an intelligent young person should spend so much time and money writing about a "shady character," when there were so many really worthwhile people. John Sohn, a contemporary of Calamity Jane, said that he wished now he had gone to her funeral, since she has become so famous. It would not have been much of an effort, he remarked, since the procession went right by his door, but then she had seemed unimportant and he had not wanted to take time from his work.

In spite of contemporary opinion of Calamity Jane, she produced an illusion on subsequent generations that has made her into a glorious character. Later writers have called her "The West's Joan of Arc,"[4] the "Black Hills Florence Nightingale,"[5] and "Lady Robinhood."[6] To what extent such glorification is justified will appear in the various chapters of this study.

For assistance in collecting material for this study the author is indebted to many people. Among those are Mrs. Anne McDonnell, former Librarian at the Historical Society of Montana (Helena); Mrs. Mabelle Patrick, Reference Librarian at the South Dakota State Historical Society (Pierre); and Miss Mae Cody, State Historian at the Wyoming State Library (Cheyenne). For helpful suggestions in writing and correcting this material I am most grateful for invaluable help given by the late Dr. Paul C. Phillips and Dr. Melvin C. Wren, formerly of the Department of History, Montana State University.

---

[4] See title of Marie Augspurger's book in footnote two.

[5] Edwin Legrand Sabin, *Wild Men in the Wild West*, p. 339.

[6] "Calamity Jane as a Lady Robinhood," *Literary Digest*, November 14, 1925, p. 46.

Main Street, Deadwood, South Dakota, 1877 (F. Jay Haynes, photographer, Haynes Foundation Collection, Montana Historical Society Photograph Archives)

On October 16, 1926, the New York *Tribune* printed this illustration of Calamity Jane rescuing the ambushed Deadwood Stage. Newspaper accounts contradicted Calamity's claim to this particular fame, although many writers have repeated the story as told in her autobiography. (Montana Historical Society Library)

INTRODUCTION
By James D. McLaird

"Long ago somebody asked me, 'Who was Calamity Jane?'" wrote Robert J. Casey in 1949, "and the answer was simple. I had the legend pat, complete with names, dates, addresses and bibliography." However, upon completion of a short biography of the famous woman for *The Black Hills and Their Incredible Characters*, Casey concluded, "today if anyone were to ask me the same question the answer would still be simple: 'I don't know.'"[1] He faced a typical problem. John S. McClintock, a Black Hills pioneer who knew Calamity Jane, complained of the same difficulty. "Numerous fictitious and unreasonable, though amusing, stories have been written concerning the life of Martha Cannary, commonly known as 'Calamity Jane.' It is difficult to cull from this mass of fiction the real facts."[2]

McClintock and Casey might have responded differently had Roberta Sollid's *Calamity Jane: A Study in Historical Criticism* been available to them. More than forty years have passed since Sollid trekked across the plains researching the life of Calamity Jane and analyzing newly discovered evidence. Yet her book, originally published in 1958 and reprinted here for the first time, remains today the most important study of the famous and notorious frontier woman. No better comment on the importance of the book can be made. Sollid's meticulous analysis of records and critical comparisons of contradictory accounts reveal a Calamity Jane far removed from the romanticized figure other writers introduced in preceding decades, and her study continues today to provide a needed corrective.

---

[1] Robert J. Casey, *The Black Hills and Their Incredible Characters* (Indianapolis: Bobbs-Merrill Company, 1949), 175.

[2] John S. McClintock, *Pioneers Days in the Black Hills: Accurate History and Facts Related by One of the Early Day Pioneers*, ed. Edward L. Senn (Deadwood, S. D.: John S. McClintock, 1939), 115. The spelling of Canary is various but appears Canary (one "n") in official documents such as United States Census records, except for her autobiography, which she narrated but probably did not write.

At the time Sollid began her study in the late 1940s, nearly fifty years had passed since Calamity's death in 1903. Yet no satisfactory biography was available. Even during Calamity's lifetime, it had been difficult to sift fact from fiction. Dime novels brought her national publicity but created an obviously fictional character bearing little resemblance to the woman met in the streets in northern plains towns. Although few people were deceived into believing the dime novel stories, Martha Canary confused the record considerably herself when she published the *Life and Adventures of Calamity Jane, By Herself* in 1896. In it, she narrated stirring adventures that were repeated regularly in books and articles about her. Calamity claimed that she served as a scout for Generals George A. Custer and George Crook; that she captured Jack McCall, the assassin of Wild Bill Hickok, by cornering him in a butcher shop with a meat cleaver; that she acted in the capacity of pony express rider; and that she saved the Deadwood stage after Indians killed the driver, Johnny Slaughter. The public learned of her birth in Princeton, Missouri, in 1852, and of the origin of her famous nickname, which she said was given her when she saved a gallant Captain James Egan during the Indian wars. Upon recovering, Egan "laughingly said: 'I name you Calamity Jane, the heroine of the plains.'"[3]

While some writers disputed her claims, Calamity continued to relate them in "wild west shows" and, undoubtedly, in bars, and peddled copies of her autobiography while traveling from town to town. Her stories became the basis of considerable fame beyond that accorded her simply for bearing the name of the dime novel heroine. Additionally, her generous sharing of whatever means she had with anyone who needed help and her unselfish caring for the ill on numerous occasions resulted in favorable comment from her contemporaries, who often suggested that her faults, which were considerable, should be forgiven in light of her virtues. Nevertheless, her dissolute behavior, including drunken sprees and alcoholism, her liaisons with numerous male

---

[3] *Life and Adventures of Calamity Jane, By Herself* (N.p.: n.d., ca. 1896).

companions called "husbands" whom she regularly deserted, her occasional prostitution, and her generally disruptive activities caused some to conclude as did one contemporary, "the veil of oblivion should be drawn over the career of that woman."[4]

Instead, approximately twenty years after Calamity Jane's death in 1903, numerous writers related increasingly exaggerated stories and created a truly legendary heroine. Titles suggest the nature of the contents: "A Wild West Heroine The Movies Overlook"; "Calamity Jane as a Lady Robin Hood" and "Calamity Jane and the Lady Wildcats."[5] Although few of these writers disputed her wayward life and rough manners, virtually all of them made her more heroic. Often, her bizarre way of life was attributed to her misfortune of being left an orphan in the West. Stories circulated that she was the fallen daughter of a Baptist minister, and even worse, that her mother might have operated the notorious brothel known as Madam Canary's "Bird Cage." Many writers concluded that frontier conditions required normally unacceptable behavior, such as the wearing of male clothing. Accounts of her misbehavior, such as her accompanying a military expedition only to be discovered and sent back when she swam nude one day with the soldiers, were colorfully related. But most frequently her faults were more than adequately forgiven due to her good deeds.

Calamity, various writers in the 1920s asserted, robbed a grocery store at gun point when sick miners needed food and there was no money to pay for it. She robbed a visitor to a house of prostitution when he lay drunk on the floor, but was released by the judge when she admitted her theft and explained how she used the cash to pay the expenses of

---

[4] Judge W. L. Kuykendall, *Frontier Days: A True Narrative of Striking Events on the Western Frontier* (N.p.: J. M. and H. L. Kuykendall, Publishers, 1917), 191. The author served as judge in Deadwood in 1876 at the trial of Jack McCall, the assassin of Wild Bill Hickok.

[5] Josiah M. Ward, "A Wild West Heroine the Movies Overlook," New York *Tribune*, October 16, 1921, p. V:5; "Calamity Jane as a Lady Robin Hood," *The Literary Digest*, November 14, 1925, pp. 46–47; and, Duncan Aikman, *Calamity Jane and the Lady Wildcats* (New York: Henry Holt and Company, 1927).

a poor girl in the hospital. Most importantly, according to one account, during the Deadwood smallpox epidemic of 1878, she tended the sick "day and night" and for week after week ministered to their wants or soothed the pillow for the dying youth whose mother or sweetheart perhaps was watching and waiting for the one never to return. It made no difference to her, that she knew them not, or that no gold would there be to repay her for the labor, the sacrifice, the danger. They were fellow beings in distress and needed help.[6]

By the 1930s, the exaggerations reached incredible dimensions. In *Wild Bill and His Era*, William Elsey Connelley compared Calamity Jane to Queen Elizabeth and Catherine the Great, both of whom, he said, "would have understood and liked plain Calamity Jane. For she was of their own type. . . . Such women as these loom together in force and character against the back drop of time!"[7] Not surprisingly, novelists who dealt with Calamity Jane were equally creative, and the conclusion of Ethel Hueston's 1937 biography, *Calamity Jane of Deadwood Gulch*, depicts the heavenly ascension of the frontierswoman at her death.[8] Such romanticized fare appealed to Hollywood, and Calamity Jane was featured with Wild Bill Hickok in *The Plainsman* in 1936, with Jean Arthur and Gary Cooper playing the leading roles. A contemporary Montana newspaper commented, "although the pioneers do not agree in their estimations of 'Calamity' they are generally agreed that the 'Calamity' Jane presented by the film makers is definitely not a life-like

[6] For most of these stories, see Jesse Brown and A. M. Willard, *The Black Hills Trails: A History of the Struggles of the Pioneers in the Winning of the Black Hills*, ed. John T. Milek (Rapid City, S. D.: Rapid City Journal Company, 1924), 411–18. See also Thomas Henderson Brown *The Romance of Everyday Life* (Mitchell, S.D.: Educator Supply Company, 1923), 41–43; and, Aikman, *Calamity Jane and the Lady Wildcats*, 42, 76.

[7] William Elsey Connelley, *Wild Bill and His Era: The Life and Adventures of James Butler Hickok* (New York: Press of the Pioneers, 1933), 197.

[8] Ethel Hueston, *Calamity Jane of Deadwood Gulch* (Indianapolis: Bobbs-Merrill Company, 1937), 306. Phoebe, the novel's main character, comments at the book's end: "'The angels, . . . are going to be surprised when she gets there.'" (p. 306).

Jean Arthur starred as Calamity Jane opposite Gary Cooper's Wild Bill Hickok in
The Plainsman in 1936. (Courtesy Paul Andrew Hutton)

portrait."[9] Indeed, it was not, but Hollywood did no worse than much of the "non-fiction" being published during the same period.

If all this were not enough, a Billings woman named Jean McCormick Hickok appeared on "We the People," a CBS network program airing on national radio in 1941, and claimed to be the daughter of Calamity Jane and Wild Bill Hickok. McCormick produced a "Diary" and accompanying correspondence by Calamity Jane to prove her assertions. Despite considerable hesitation by historians to accept these claims, McCormick's story often appeared in new publications about Calamity Jane, with "Diary" entries included in the chronological narrative of her life.[10] Researchers who thought McCormick's documents were fraudulant faced a formidable problem: there was no acceptable account of Calamity's life for comparison. It was this vacuous condition that allowed uninterrupted growth of the legends for more than twenty years.

When the Calamity Jane legend reached its peak in the 1940s, it finally provoked hostile response. Numerous historians joined the debunking effort. Harold E. Briggs's essay, "The Calamity Jane Myth," published first in 1940, was the most emphatic early attack. Decrying recent portrayals of Calamity "as a picturesque and romantic border character, a 'heroine of the plains,'" Briggs concluded that much of Calamity's own *Life and Adventures* "must be regarded as a fabrication of her imagination." Briggs suggested that "a modern psychologist would find much of interest in the

---

[9] Walter Ed Taylor, unidentified newspaper clipping dated August 5, 1937, vertical file, Montana Historical Society, Helena, Montana. The reviewer added that Calamity Jane "was never the peaches and cream sweetheart shown in 'The Plainsman.'"

[10] Billings *Gazette*, June 15, 1941. On historians' hesitation to accept McCormick's claims, see Clarence S. Paine, "She Laid Her Pistol Down; or, The Last Will and Testament of Calamity Jane," *The Westerners Brand Book 1944* (Chicago, Ill.: Westerners, 1946), 21. Paine investigated the documents for perhaps a decade. After discovering several obvious errors, he concluded: "if the diary is a forgery, it is either the cleverest or the most bungled attempt of which I know." An example of a popular article accepting the diary is Kathryn Wright, "The *Real* Calamity Jane," *True West*, 5 (November-December, 1957), 22–25, 41–42.

glamour with which Jane, in her later years, overlaid the drab adventures of her youth, when her only claim to fame was her absolute lack of respectability." Sensational tales by more recent writers, Briggs added, "are outside the realm of possibility, and no contemporary will vouch for them."[11]

Briggs's short sketch, included in the midst of his massive *Frontiers of the Northwest*, reached few readers interested specifically in Calamity Jane. It established a tone, however, for ensuing writers. The need for a sound biography was apparent, and several full-length studies were in preparation. J. Leonard Jennewein, Lloyd McFarling, Nolie Mumey, Clarence Paine, and Roberta Beed Sollid all were pursuing elusive documents actively, and most of these writers were interested in debunking the legends.[12] McFarling never completed his work, however, and Paine published three short accounts but no book. Mumey compiled documents, including the spurious McCormick "Diary," and published them without critical comment. Jennewein decided a complete biography was beyond his means at that time and instead published a pamphlet assessing Calamity's character and establishing the inaccuracy of several tales about her then circulating.

Only Roberta Sollid completed an extensive manuscript that was published. Beginning her study of Calamity Jane under the direction of history professor Paul Phillips at what was then Montana State University in Missoula, Sollid finished her master's thesis on the famous woman in 1951. Seven years later, the Montana Historical Society edited and published her thesis as a book-length biography.

---

[11]Harold E. Briggs, *Frontiers of the Northwest: A History of the Upper Missouri Valley* (New York: Peter Smith, 1950), 75, 78, 79. Briggs's book was first published in 1940 by D. Appleton-Century Company.

[12]J. Leonard Jennewein, *Calamity Jane of the Western Trails* (Huron, S.D.: Dakota Books, 1953), 5, mentions consideration of a full-length biography. Lloyd McFarling's draft of a biography resides in the South Dakota State Historical Society, Pierre, South Dakota. Nolie Mumey, *Calamity Jane* (Denver: Range Press, 1950), is an uncritical work that reprinted numerous articles as well as the controversial "Diary and Letters." Clarence Paine published two additional essays: "Calamity Jane: Man? Woman? or Both?," *Westerners Brand Book 1945–46* (Chicago, Ill.: Westerners, 1947), 69–82; and, "Wild Bill Hickok and Calamity Jane," in *The Black Hills*, ed. Roderick Peattie (New York: Vanguard Press, 1952), 151–76.

That Sollid's work shared the debunking atmosphere in response to recent legend-making is evident in the author's opening comments. While Calamity "gained notoriety and a certain amount of fame as a character, enough at least so that the newspapers mentioned her when she was in town," she was, Sollid noted, "all but forgotten" for twenty years after her death. Then, she added, "for some unknown reason, sensation-writers and historians began to take an interest in her." Publications about Calamity were much in demand, and "prodigious quantities of material containing a paucity of truth were written about her," Sollid wrote. "She became the heroine of many a tale that found ready sale during the 1920s and 1930s. If facts were not known, they were invented. No one could prove them false."[13]

It was Sollid's intent to sift through and sort the legends, using contemporary newspaper records and other documents to separate "the folklore and legend of her life from established facts." Documenting her life was difficult because few records survived, but newspapers at least established Calamity's "whereabouts on or near a particular date." Enough of these dates Sollid argued, "indicate a pattern or trend which may be used to determine the truth of her own stories or of those repeated by other people." That Sollid generally rejected unverifiable stories is apparent in her comment regarding the fifty people she interviewed for her thesis, of whom only "about ten can be credited with dependable contributions."[14]

In 1949, Sollid traveled through the northern plains states, visited historical societies and libraries, and tracked down elusive documents. Bert Hall, a rancher and author,

[13] Roberta Beed Sollid, *Calamity Jane: A Study in Historical Criticism* (Helena: Western Press/Historical Society of Montana, 1958), xi.

[14] Ibid., xi–xii.

[15] Bert Hall, *Roundup Years, Old Muddy to Black Hills* (Pierre, S.D.: State Publishing Co., 1954), 345. Robert Sollid remembered Pierre as the hottest place she had ever been. Expecting to work on Friday at the historical society, she became understandably nervous when the governor announced that the staff could have the day off because it was his birthday. Fortunately, the staff was compassionate, and the rules were less restrictive than would be found in modern times: she was allowed to work alone in the library! Interview with Roberta Beed Sollid, September 29, 1994.

recalled Sollid as a young woman riding a bus from Vivian, South Dakota, to Pierre in the middle of the night. "On the bus that had come from Rapid City," he said, "was a comely young lady who joined the conveyance going north. With little else to do on the 35 mile ride, I struck up a brief conversation with her just before we disembarked in front of the Waverly hotel." When he learned she was going to the historical society as he was, Hall "naturally asked her special topic of research. She replied coyly, 'I'm ashamed to tell you, I'm looking for information on Calamity Jane.'"[15]

Sollid's embarrassment derived from the nature of her subject's reputation. In the Black Hills, she explained, the "older generation were not pleased to know that further research was being made on such a person as Calamity Jane." They believed Calamity was "of no consequence" and "expressed surprise that an intelligent young person should spend so much time and money writing about a 'shady character,' when there were so many really worthwhile people."[16] Unlike previous biographers, Sollid quickly concluded that Calamity Jane had few heroic qualities. The opening sentence of her published account declared: "No career is so elusive to the historian as that of a loose woman. Calamity Jane was that sort of woman. Like most prostitutes and drunkards she left little behind in the way of tangible evidence which could be used by historians to reconstruct the story of her checkered career."[17] Other writers, when weighing Calamity's good and bad qualities, concluded that her virtues were in the ascendancy. Sollid was of the opposite persuasion. While she admitted Calamity had a heart of gold, helped the sick, and had admirable qualities of character such as not being guilty of hypocrisy, Sollid believed "drunkenness, whoring and violence" were dominant in Calamity's life. With this in mind, she asked readers to judge for themselves "whether the mild qualities should outweigh the more dominant ones."[18]

---

[16]Sollid, *Calamity Jane*, xiii.

[17] Ibid., xi.

[18] Ibid., 124.

Like other debunkers, Sollid found the particulars of Calamity Jane's *Adventures* easy prey. Calamity could not have been a scout for Custer at the time and place she suggested because the famous general was not in the vicinity. Calamity's claim to have saved the Deadwood stage when Johnny Slaughter was killed was without foundation; outlaws, not Indians, killed the stage driver, and contemporary newspapers provided detailed accounts of the passengers and arrival of the stage without mention of the notorious woman. Calamity's account of the capture of Jack McCall could not be substantiated in contemporary newspapers, which left Calamity unmentioned when recounting the story.

In addition to showing *Life and Adventures* inaccurate, Sollid introduced numerous new contemporary sources, especially newspaper articles, that enabled her to establish a more authentic portrayal of Calamity and allowed her to reject many tall tales. Sollid also used comparative analysis when critically examining reminiscences and discovered plagiarism between accounts by Harry "Sam" Young and Valentine T. McGillycuddy. She criticized Estelline Bennett's highly acclaimed *Old Deadwood Days* for muddying the historical record by combining a newspaper story of Calamity's unauthorized buggy ride to Fort Laramie in 1876 with a tale of her coming into the Black Hills in 1875 with General Crook. She wondered aloud why, if Calamity Jane nursed hundreds of victims, the Deadwood newspapers did not "'sing her praises' during the times when the smallpox epidemics struck Deadwood," and thus questioned Jesse Brown and A. M. Willard's generally accepted story in *Black Hills Trails* about Calamity's supposed efforts to help the sick in 1878. Regarding Duncan Aikman's story of Martha Canary's parents, Robert and Charlotte, in Princeton, Missouri, Sollid queried why the land sales records Aikman cited could not be located, implying he had invented the entire tale. Other legends, such as that of Calamity Jane "rolling" the drunken visitor to a house of prostitution to pay a poor woman's hospital bill, were "without any authentication," but Sollid argued, "repeated so often that it is often believed."[19]

19 Ibid., 6–7, 11–12, 32, 65, 89.

Calamity Jane posed with army soldiers guarding the Northern Pacific Railway in Billings, Montana, during the Pullman railroad strike of 1894. (Montana Historical Society Photograph Archives)

Despite Sollid's efforts and those of other debunkers, persistent repetition of legends—and even creation of new tales—continued after publication of her thesis. When writers spawned new versions of the legendary adventures of the frontier heroine, Sollid joined other historians in trying to prevent their acceptance. She responded harshly, for example, when Glenn Clairmonte's *Calamity Was the Name for Jane* (1959)—a biography advertised as non-fiction but replete with legends, a mixing of fact and fantasy, and invented conversations—uncritically accepted the "Diary and Letters of Calamity Jane." "There is more misinformation found here per square page," Sollid wrote, "than in most western fiction novels dealing with the much publiciz-ed Calamity Jane, a well-meaning but good-for-nothing frontierswoman." She denounced the use of McCormick's "Diary and Letters," which she said, "contains so much that is contradictory with known facts that it may be completely discredited." In the debunking tradition, Sollid concluded that Clairmonte's book was historical fiction, or "story telling," not biography. Of Clarimonte's nickname "darning needle," derived from the author's reputation for careful research, Sollid asserted: "the darning needle dropped its first stitch on page one and had failed to pick it up by the time it reached the last page, fifteen chapters later." Sollid suggested "embroidery needle" would be a better sobriquet, based on Clairmonte's ability to embroider colorful conversations and situations.[20]

By contrast, when Sollid's biography was published in 1958, scholars greeted her efforts positively, and reviews of her book were generally favorable. "Out of the mass of evidence she has done her best to pass intelligent judgment on the various stories that have been published," wrote Robert Riegel of Sollid's *Calamity Jane*, and "the results are not happy for the romanticist. The great majority of the stories are rejected as obviously fictional, with most of the remainder labeled at least partly false or else doubtful."[21] Fellow

[20]Glenn Clairmonte, *Calamity Was the Name for Jane* (Denver: Sage Books, 1959). For Sollid's review of Cairmonte's book, see *Montana The Magazine of Western History*, 10 (July 1960), 70.

[21]For Robert Riegel's review of Sollid's *Calamity Jane*, see *Montana The Magazine of Western History*, 9 (January 1959), 63–64.

Calamity Jane authority, J. Leonard Jennewein, concluded that Sollid's work was the "most valuable published on Calamity."[22]

Despite Sollid's critical analysis and discovery of new sources, which enabled her to rescue a more accurate portrayal of Calamity Jane from that of legend and sensationalism, she made several significant errors that left her task incomplete and allowed confusion in the record. Her attack on the unreliability of Harry "Sam" Young, whose account was plagiarized by McGillycuddy, prompted Sollid to question whether Calamity accompanied the Black Hills expedition of 1875 as they claimed. She disputed Young's claim to having been a bartender in Deadwood when Wild Bill Hickok was killed and suggested that because Young appears in no historical records he probably fabricated his western adventures. In fact, contemporary newspapers and other documents show Young to have been a teamster in 1874–1875, as he suggested, and a bartender in Deadwood in 1876. Calamity's presence with the expedition in 1875, moreover, is now proven. Similarly, the Missouri land records cited by Duncan Aikman, the existence of which Sollid questioned, did indeed exist. Sollid's laudable critical analysis occasionally caused her to condemn authentic, if occasionally exaggerated, accounts.[23]

While discovering an array of new information, Sollid failed to locate a number of important documents that might

---

[22]J. Leonard Jennewein, *Calamity Jane of the Western Trails*, 4th ed. (Rapid City, S.D.: Dakota West Books, 1991), 46. The Sollid and Jennewein studies are listed as the two most important studies of Calamity Jane in Howard R. Lamar, ed., *Reader's Encyclopedia of the American West* (New York: Thomas Y. Crowell Company, 1977), 147.

[23]Calamity Jane's presence with the Black Hills Expedition of 1875 was noted by "Mac," the correspondent for the Chicago *Inter-Ocean*, in his dispatch, July 3, 1875. That Harry "Sam" Young was a bullwhacker at this time is documented in the account book of John Hunton reproduced in William Francis Hooker, *The Bullwhacker: Adventures of a Frontier Freighter* (Yonkers-on-Hudson, N. Y.: World Book Company, 1924), 163. While bartending in Mann & Lewis' Saloon "No. 10" in Deadwood, Young mistakingly shot Myer Baum, thinking Baum was "Laughing Sam" Hartman, shortly after Hickok's death. Details were reported in the Deadwood *Black Hills Pioneer*, August 26, 1876. Copies of records relating land purchases and sales by the Canary family in Mercer County, Missouri, can be found in the Clarence S. Paine Papers, Center for Western Studies, Augustana College, Sioux Falls, South Dakota.

have improved her study. The 1860 census records from Mercer County, Missouri, for example, list Martha with her parents, Robert and Charlotte, and a special Wyoming census taken in 1869 shows Calamity to be in Piedmont, Wyoming, alone, as she related in her *Life and Adventures*. Several errors in Sollid's story also derived from missed newspaper articles. She incorrectly concluded, for example, that Calamity did not make it from Minneapolis to Chicago during her 1896 dime museum tour. Having examined the Chicago *Tribune* with no result, Sollid decided Calamity must have been fired before reaching Chicago because of her disruptive behavior while drunk. In fact, the Chicago *Inter-Ocean* carried a front-page interview of Calamity, an interview that provided additional insights into her personality. Sollid compounded such normal problems of research and interpretation by misreading at least one document: records touting the arrest of Calamity Jane and Charles Townley in 1888 for fornication. Sollid concluded these records involved Calamity when they actually pertained to a different woman, identified by newspapers at the time as "Calamity Jane No. 2." The woman's real name was Annie Filmore.[24]

Every book errs in some details, and discovery of additional documents clarifying the story are to be expected. With minor exceptions, Sollid's use of contemporary documents concerning Calamity Jane for a "study in historical criticism" was immensely successful. Nevertheless, her topical approach failed to portray fully Calamity Jane's personality, activities, and movements. As reviewer Robert Riegel observed: "Mrs. Sollid aims not so much at telling the life story of Calamity Jane Cannary as at trying to discover the truthfulness of the various tales told about her."[25] Developing her study topically, with chapters on bull-whacking, scouting, Calamity's nickname, "husbands," gunwoman, jail, and

---

[24]Census of 1860, Mercer County, Missouri; Census of 1869, Piedmont, Wyoming Territory; Chicago *Inter-Ocean*, January 28, 1896. For court records of the Annie Fillmore-Charles Townly arrest, see the Livingston, Montana, *Enterprise*, November 10, 11, 1888.

[25]Riegel, review of Sollid's *Calamity Jane*, 63–64.

nursing, Sollid failed to develop a chronological framework sufficiently adequate to assess certain reminiscences and legends. Paucity of contemporary records—especially between 1880 and 1895 and again between 1896 and 1901—combined with tales inaccurately set during these periods to make Calamity Jane seem to pop up randomly in various locations throughout the northern plains. Insufficient evidence also disallowed an explanation concerning how a relatively obscure Calamity Jane became the subject of dime novels. Every account since the publication of Sollid's book shares these defects, opening the door for inclusion of inaccurate tales and impossible memoirs, and encouraging the assumption that Calamity's daredevil deeds must have brought her the noteworthy contemporary fame that led to the attention of dime novel writers. Also, the inaccuracy of McCormick's "Diary" could not be proven, for there were too few established dates for comparison. While Sollid was certain it was fraudulant, she could not provide evidence that would put the matter to rest.

Despite these problems, the flaws in Sollid's *Calamity Jane* are minor compared to those of published accounts of the frontier woman appearing before and after Sollid's biography. Sollid not only produced the finest study of Calamity yet in print, she also pointed the way for future research by showing that contemporary documents existed with which historians could establish a firm basis for assessing unreliable reminiscences and embellished tales. This corrective approach to the romanticized Calamity Jane of the early twentieth century was an invaluable contribution. Published in a limited edition of 2,000 copies, however, Sollid's study soon became inaccessible to the general reader. Deserving a wider audience, this reprint is a welcome respite from continued appearances of the legendary heroine in history, popular literature, and film.

Chapter I.

CALAMITY IN BRIEF

Martha Cannary was born sometime in the late 1840's or early 1850's in the Middle West, perhaps in Missouri or Iowa. While she was still a young girl her family migrated to Montana Territory. She and her younger brothers and sisters were neglected by their worthless parents who either died or deserted their young family. Martha was compelled to forage for herself and chose the easiest path. In her life of shame she associated with the lowest types of miners, soldiers and railroad workers. During the early days of the gold rush in the Black Hills, having somewhere in the meantime acquired the name of Calamity Jane,[1] she made herself conspicuous by her immorality and also by her kindness to the sick and unfortunate. For fifteen years or more she roamed over the Dakotas, Colorado, Montana and Wyoming, spending considerable time drunk or in jail. She accumulated numerous "husbands", by whom she may have borne children. Her more commendable activities included spasmodic periods of bull-whacking, at which she was adept, running a hurdy-gurdy house and a saloon, staking a few claims, and waiting on tables in restaurants. Later she returned to Deadwood, South Dakota, where temporarily she was welcomed by many respectable citizens who had known her in the days of '76. At two different times she appeared in dime museums in the East, but was unable to keep those jobs because of her riotous behavior. In 1896, she published a highly fictionalized story of her life and sold the little pamphlet as a means of partial support. Using some of her amorous escapades with the soldiers as background, she told in her *Auto-*

---

[1] The nickname Calamity Jane was often shortened to Calamity or Calam.

1

biography[2] heroic tales of her scouting with the army. The last few years of her life she spent in a pathetic state of almost perpetual drunkenness. She died in Terry, South Dakota, August 1, 1903, a lonely broken old woman. The oldtimers and curious newcomers to Deadwood turned out to give her one of the biggest funerals the community had ever had. People seemed willing to forget her sordid life and to remember her sunny disposition.

Such, in brief, is the story of Calamity Jane. Considering the very minor role she played in the winning of the West and the small influence she had on society, this account is as detailed as she probably deserves. It is in an effort to separate fact from fiction and to appraise the importance of this strange woman that the following analysis is presented.

---

[2] This pamphlet, entitled *Life and Adventures of Calamity Jane, by Herself* (Mrs. M. Burk), is frequently quoted in this study. When quoting it, spelling, punctuation and language are given precisely as in the original. The first edition was published in 1896 but neither date nor the publisher and place of publication are mentioned. In footnotes the reference will be cited merely as *Autobiography*. (Editor's Note: Reproduced on the following two pages are the title page and the signature page of the Autobiography as it was originally published. The full text is printed in the Appendix of this book.)

LIFE AND ADVENTURES

—of—

Calamity ✳ Jane,

BY HERSELF.

My maiden name was Marthy Cannary, was born in Princeton, Missourri. May 1st, 1852. Father and mother natives of Ohio. Had two brothers and three sisters, I being the oldest of the children. As a child I always had a fondness for adventure and out-door exercise and especial fondness for horses which I began to ride at an early age and continued to do so until I became an expert rider being able to ride the most vicious and stubborn of horses, in fact the greater portion of my life in early times was spent in this manner.

In 1865 we emigrated from our homes in Missourri by the overland route to Virginia City, Montana, taking five months to make the journey. While on the way the greater portion of my time was spent in hunting along with the men and hunters of the party, in fact I was at all times with the men when there was excitement and adventures to be had. By the time we reached Virginia City I was considered a remarkable good shot and a fearless rider for a girl of my age. I remember many occurrences on the journey from Missourri to Montana. Many times in crossing the mountains the conditions of the trail were

— 7 —.

Scout who was made so famous through her daring career in the West and Black Hill countries.

An agent of Kohl & Middleton, the celebrated Museum men came to Deadwood, through the solicitation of the gentleman whom I had met there and arrangements were made to place me before the public in this manner. My first engagement began at the Palace Museum, Minneapolis, January 20th, 1896, under Kohl and Middleton's management.

Hoping that this little history of my life may interest all readers, I remain as in the older days,

Yours,

MRS. M. BURK, (*Dorsett*

BETTER KNOWN AS CALAMITY JANE

(ca. 1896)

Chapter II.

BIRTH

There have been two equally popular and disputed versions of the birth of Calamity Jane. The first story, her own, is that she was born in Princeton, Missouri, as Martha Cannary in 1852. The second is that she was born as Jane Dalton at Fort Laramie, Wyoming, in 1860.

It is undoubtedly due to the support of a most distinguished gentleman, Dr. V. T. McGillycuddy, that the Dalton story early gained numerous exponents, among whom were reputable historians. Dr. McGillycuddy, a physician, was the topographer on the Jenney Expedition into the Black Hills in 1875, and afterwards became a well-known Indian agent. Perhaps it was because of the good work he did in his various positions, and because he was well-liked in general, that his words were accepted as fact when, in later life, he told and wrote of his past experiences.

In a letter which he wrote to the editor of the *Rapid City Journal* in October, 1924, McGillycuddy gave an account of Calamity Jane's life from birth up to the time he claimed he met her on the Jenney Expedition. His biographical sketch in part reads:

> She was born at Fort Laramie in 1860, the daughter of an enlisted soldier named Dalton, and he was discharged from the army in 1861, and with his wife and daughter settled on a ranch on a stream called the La Bontie about 120 miles northwest of Laramie beyond Ft. Fetterman. In the fall of that year a war party of Sioux Indians raided that district killing everyone in their path, among them Dalton. Mrs. Dalton was shot in the eye with an arrow, destroying the sight, removing the arrow with her own hand, she placed her one year old

5

daughter on her back and escaped. Traveling nights
and hiding by day, subsisting on weeds and roots,
she finally managed to reach Ft. Laramie in eight
days, a mere skeleton of her former self, her clothing
in shreds, and in a short time expired.[1]

From this sketch or perhaps from other correspondence between McGillycuddy and Mr. Doane Robinson, Secretary of the South Dakota Historical Society,
Mr. Robinson believed the Dalton story. A year later
he repeated the story to Dr. Grace Hebard, then professor of political economics at the University of Wyoming.[2] He also repeated it to others, and invariably
cited McGillycuddy as his authority. In this way the
Dalton story spread.

McGillycuddy's notes were left to his wife who used
them in a book entitled, *McGillycuddy Agent*. In this
book published twenty-four years after her husband
had written his account of Calamity Jane, she developed
the story in much greater detail than had the topographer. She explained that her husband had obtained
the information from Colonel R. I. Dodge. Colonel
Dodge related that he learned of it when he first came
to Fort Laramie where Calamity had been living for
fourteen years.[3]

The Dodge-McGillycuddy version of Calamity Jane's
origin breaks down when compared to the fantastic
memoirs published in 1915 by a Mr. Harry "Sam"
Young, who claimed to have been a teamster with the
Jenney Expedition.[4] Comparison of the two accounts
reveals beyond contradiction that McGillycuddy's letter of 1924 was copied from the Young narrative published nine years earlier. Mrs. McGillycuddy's story of
Calamity Jane can also be traced to "Sam" Young's

---

[1] Dr. V. T. McGillycuddy to Editor of the *Rapid City Journal*, October 1,
1924, South Dakota Historical Society Library.
[2] Mr. Doane Robinson to Dr. Grace Hebard, November 6, 1925, South
Dakota Historical Society Library.
[3] Julia B. McGillycuddy, *McGillycuddy Agent*, pp. 25-27.
[4] Harry "Sam" Young *Hard Knocks*, pp. 171-172.

narrative. Both these accounts repeat the Dalton tale in words almost identical with those used by Young. Except for a few commas and an occasional phrase like a "war party of Sioux" instead of a "large body of Sioux" or "removing the arrow with her own hand" instead of "with her own hand extracted the arrow," the sentences are the same.[5] Many other incidents narrated by the McGillycuddys in both the letter and the book are taken verbatim from Young's book. These show that McGillycuddy was not the real author of the Dalton story. The whole thing becomes even more unreliable when it is found that most of Young's material is contrary to accepted history. For example, Young gloats over his prestige of having been the bartender in the Saloon No. 10 when Wild Bill Hickok was killed. It is common knowledge among Deadwood citizens that Anson Tippie was the bartender at the fatal shooting of Hickok, so Young becomes an impostor on that score. Both Young and McGillycuddy agree in almost exact words that Jane Dalton was adopted by Sergeant Bassett and his wife, who called the child Calamity Jane, because of the calamity which had befallen her as a baby. According to Young, "She was the pet of the fort with no particular use for a citizen, but anyone with a blue coat and brass buttons, could catch Calamity."[6] McGillycuddy added that "she was something like Topsy in Uncle Tom's Cabin, she was not exactly 'raised, she growed' ".[7] Much investigation among old-timers failed to give a clue of anyone who might be "Sam" Young, although this unknown author wrote as if he were an eye-witness to every event that took place in the Black Hills. The chances that these two men, both of whom wrote more than forty years after the event described and nine years apart in their own stories, would come up with accounts so much alike, are too slim to be considered.

[5] *Ibid.*, pp. 169-170.
[6] *Ibid.*, p. 170.
[7] Dr. McGillycuddy's letter cited in footnote one.

The date of Calamity Jane's birth as related by Dr. McGillycuddy was in 1860. He gave an eye-witness account of seeing her in 1875 when she was "not over sixteen."[8] If she was born in 1852 or before, he erred badly in his estimate of her age. Inquiries by this writer in the area on which he reported indicate that some of the doctor's stories suffered a loss of detailed accuracy with the passage of time. If McGillycuddy did see a bizarre sixteen-year-old girl at Fort Laramie, and Dodge told him that she was camp mascot and was born in 1860, there are three possibilities: Colonel Dodge was being bamboozled by a hardened camp follower; he was misinforming McGillycuddy; or the bizarre young girl who went on the military convoy of the Jenney Expedition was not *the* Calamity Jane, but another. Colonel Dodge's story of Calamity's birth was frankly a hearsay report. He told McGillycuddy that Calamity was at the fort when he arrived. McGillycuddy spoke later in his book of having seen a good deal of Calamity, so confusion of identity is not likely. It seems strange that the commandant of an army camp would allow a young girl to run loose on his post while he commented with a laugh that she was absolutely without morals.[9]

The only evidence given by Calamity Jane herself that she might have been Jane Dalton was a remark she once made while in a slightly tipsy condition. She called herself "the child of the regiment."[10] That title fits the reference to her as the "pet of the fort" during the years when Dodge said she stayed at Fort Laramie. But she could have been referring to other times when, as Martha Cannary, she lived around or near some of the army camps; or, maybe, it was simply drunken chatter.

[8] Julia B. McGillycuddy, p. 25.

[9] *Ibid.*, p. 27.

[10] *Cheyenne* (Wyoming) *Daily Leader*, July 7, 1877.

69. FORT LARAMIE.

FORT LARAMIE   Plate I

One version of Calamity Jane's birth has it that she was born at this Wyoming Territory fort, the daughter of an enlisted soldier named Dalton. Historians are now generally agreed that this was not true. However, this was one of several Army posts that Calamity Jane frequented. This photo was taken in 1868, and is reproduced by courtesy of the Montana Historical Society.

If, for a moment, it may be assumed that Calamity Jane was Jane Dalton, then the problems of her biographers would be greatly simplified. Jane Dalton lived at Fort Laramie from the time of her arrival at the age of one until she was fifteen or sixteen in 1875. In fact, were Jane Dalton the real Calamity Jane, the task of writing her early life is made so simple that it is no wonder so many people have fallen in line with the Jane Dalton version instead of the Martha Cannary one. If Calamity Jane had been Jane Dalton it seems that she would have admitted it, for what woman would say she was born in 1852 or earlier, if it were really 1860?

Calamity Jane's *Autobiography* gives quite a different story regarding the date and place of birth. She wrote that "My maiden name was Martha Cannary, was born in Princeton, Missouri, May 1st, 1852."[11] There is little corroborating evidence to prove or disprove her story. It is not, however, out of line with what might logically have happened. If she had presented the more interesting and breathtaking Dalton version herself, there might be a question. The matter-of-fact beginning of her own account is too plausible to doubt unless proof of something else can be provided.

Most writers have failed to notice a newspaper article which appeared in the *Montana Post* in December, 1864. This notice might help to substantiate her birth date of 1852:

> Three little girls, who state their names to be Canary, appeared at the door of Mr. Fergus, on Idaho Street, soliciting charity. The ages of the two eldest ones were about ten and twelve, respectively. The eldest girl carried in her arms her infant sister, a baby of about twelve months of age. Canary, the father, it seems, is a gambler in Nevada.[12] The

[11] See the first two paragraphs of the *Autobiography*.
[12] Nevada was a small town in Alder Gulch a few miles from Virginia City, Montana.

mother is a woman of the lowest grade, and was last seen in town, at Dr. Byam's office, a day or two since . . . We understand that the little ones returned to Nevada, where they have existed for some time.[13]

The question is, of course, whether or not the Canary family referred to in the news item is the same Cannary family of which Calamity Jane was a member. The Cannary emigration to Montana might reasonably have been in 1864 instead of 1865, which would have made it possible for Martha to have been begging in Virginia City, Montana Territory, on that cold December evening. If her claim to be the oldest of four girls was true, she would most likely have been the twelve year old who was carrying the one year old sister. If she were that girl, the date of May, 1852, would have made her twelve years old in December, 1864, when the event took place. The news item tallies with Calamity's own story so closely that it is more than probable that the two families are one and the same.

Newspaper Account	*Calamity's Account*
1 Three little sisters.	Had three sisters besides self.
2 Age of eldest about twelve.	Was eldest and would have been twelve in 1864.
3 Name was Canary.	Name was Cannary.
4 Incident was in Va. City, Mont. Terr. 1864.	Emigrated to Va. City, Mont. Terr 1865.
5 Mother and father mentioned.	Mother and father emigrated with their family.

If the article from the *Post* was about Martha Cannary, then she told much that was true in the first part of her *Autobiography.* It follows that she might have been accurate, too, when saying that she was born in Princeton, Missouri, in 1852.

On the other hand, she may have been older than she claimed to be in the *Autobiography.* She once told Lewis Freeman that she was born in 1848.[14] Her statement to a news reporter in 1887, that "it hardly seems

[13] *Montana Post* (Virginia City), December 31, 1864.
[14] Lewis R. Freeman, *Down the Yellowstone,* p. 74.

to me that I was born over forty years ago," helps to substantiate what she told Freeman.[15] Simple arithmetic from those figures would put her birth date during or before 1847. Even if she lied about her age in the *Autobiography*, the *Montana Post* data are still just as applicable to the Cannary (Calamity's) family as ever, because the three little girls begging could all have been Calamity's younger sisters. It does not take much stretch of imagination to picture Calamity Jane out reveling in all the licentious activities that the wicked mining town of Virginia City offered, while the three youngsters were turned loose to fend for themselves.

Mr. Clarence Paine, a recent biographer, found material which convinced him that Calamity Jane came from Princeton, Missouri, before she moved out West, but then he said she was born eight years prior to the time she claimed, and in Illinois, not Missouri. His evidence was the federal census of 1860 which listed an M. J. Conarray as living with Abigail Conarray, presumably Calamity's mother, in Marion Township, Mercer County, Missouri. M. J. Conarray was listed by the census-taker as being sixteen years of age and born in Illinois. A younger sister, aged seven, born in Iowa was also listed. As Paine pointed out, Martha Jane could have made a mistake in her own last name, or the census taker could have mixed up the spelling of Cannary to Conarray. While no male head of the house was listed, there did appear a seventeen-year-old farm laborer, which indicated to Paine that M. J. Conarray was probably reared on a farm.[16]

Perhaps the most widely quoted writer of Calamity Jane literature, Mr. Duncan Aikman, is certain that he located Calamity's family in Princeton and even found records that Bob Cannary, Calamity's father, bought one hundred eighty acres of farm land for five hundred

---

[15] *Cheyenne Daily Leader*, June 21, 1887.

[16] Clarence Paine, "Calamity Jane, Man? Woman? or Both?", *Westerners Brand Book*, 1945-1946, pp. 77-78.

dollars.[17] If deeds for this property ever did exist, they are not on hand at the present.[18] Aikman visited Princeton in the 1920's and from a few recollections of old-timers spun an elaborate tale of Martha Cannary and all of her family. Of special interest in this account were the parents, Bob and Charlotte. The latter he described as flamboyant, youthful and voluptuous with her unruly coppery red hair and large brown eyes which never hesitated to flirt with any man whom chance threw in her path. She smoked cigarettes and drank whisky at a time when such things were classed as a vice. By contrast, Bob was a listless fellow. According to his sister, he was dazzled by Charlotte's beauty in her early teens when he found her in an Ohio bawdy house. As an innocent and not very shrewd young farm boy he had married her to reform her, but obviously failed in his mission.[19]

John S. McClintock, Deadwood's pioneer historian who spent considerable time and money debunking western frontier characters, believed that Martha Cannary was born in Princeton. Reports received by him which he deemed authentic stated that her father was John Cannary, a hard drinker who was very abusive of his family. They moved from Missouri to Calamus, Dodge County, Wisconsin, and Martha was known to McClintock's informant as a member of the family there in 1866.[20] Either McClintock or his informant could have erred in recollecting or recording the date that the Cannary family came to Wisconsin. Their arrival might have been several years before 1866, which would give them time to migrate West and be there by December, 1864. It is not incongruous to think that the gambler in Montana referred to in the newspaper and the abusive father in Wisconsin were the same person.

[17] Duncan Aikman, *Calamity Jane and the Lady Wildcats*, p. 15.
[18] Inquiry at the County Courthouse in Princeton, Missouri, gave no clue to the records mentioned by Aikman.
[19] Aikman, pp. 7, 9.
[20] John S. McClintock, *Pioneer Days in the Black Hills*, p. 115.

While neither the newspaper account nor the points presented by Paine, Aikman and McClintock prove that part or parts of what Calamity said about her birth are true, yet there is nothing which can completely disqualify any of the evidence. With so many little related bits pointing to confirm, in part, Calamity's story, the information as she gave it is, in all probability, vaguely true. It is possible that Martha Cannary was not born in Missouri. Her family might have moved there early in her life. Then, when it came time for her to write of her birthplace, Princeton was the first clear recollection she had and consequently accurate enough to suit her.

The most interesting of the many other versions of Calamity's birth, of which none has ever become popular, is one given by Dr. A. R. Hendricks of Des Moines, Iowa. It is noted here not because of any historic importance but because Calamity, unbelievably enough, was given an ecclesiastical background. In an 1877 Cheyenne paper Dr. Hendricks claimed that he knew Calamity Jane before she acquired her epithet. He said that he knew her people well, especially her father, B. W. Coombs who for many years was a pastor of the First Baptist Church in Burlington, Iowa. There she was born in 1847, the youngest of four children, with two brothers and one sister.[21]

Someone must have taken the story seriously, for the following year a Black Hills writer said that Calamity Jane was indignant over the reports that she was "a 'horse thief,' a 'highway woman,' a 'three-card monte sharp' and a 'minister's daughter.' She says all these are false, the last especially."[22] Fifty years later

---

[21] *Cheyenne* (Wyoming) *Sun,* July 7, 1877. This particular article must have had wide publicity because the same one appeared in the *New Northwest* (Deer Lodge, Montana), September 7, 1877 and the *Black Hills Weekly Champion* (Central City, South Dakota), July 16, 1877.

[22] Horatio N. Maguire, *The Coming Empire,* p. 64.

the same quote was juggled to read that "she was variously referred to as a 'highway woman,' a 'three-card monte sharp' and a 'minister's daughter.' Jane said all these statements were all false, except the last which is authentic."[23]

---

[23] "Calamity Jane as a Lady Robinhood," *Literary Digest,* November 14, 1925, p. 46.

Chapter III.

APPEARANCE

Calamity Jane's early life from the time she came to Montana until the mid-1870's is almost entirely unknown. Her own words about this period, however, deserve attention as there may be some truth in them. She says in her *Autobiography* that her family took five months to make the journey by the Overland Route from Missouri to Montana. There is nothing strange in that statement. Hundreds were leaving their homes to seek gold or claim land in the West. The journey was arduous, and the Cannarys probably did spend five months traveling through Nebraska, Wyoming, Utah, Idaho and Montana to Virginia City. It is not difficult to imagine that a vivacious girl of the young immigrant's temperament enjoyed hunting, riding and the other experiences which she described, if allowance is made for her insistence upon being the heroine in all the adventures. She observes in her story that "many times in crossing the mountains the conditions of the trail were so bad that we frequently had to lower the wagons over ledges by hand with ropes."[1] Other writers have related that pioneers trekking west over the mountains did that very thing.

Martha's parents did not long survive the trip west, and her family ties were soon broken. According to the *Autobiography*,[2] the mother died in 1866 and was buried in Blackfoot, Montana.[3] Martha tells nothing more of her life in this period but one incident is related by Tom Brown in his book, *Romance of Everyday Life.*

---

[1] *Autobiography*, pp. 1-2.

[2] *Ibid.*, p. 2. See first half of second paragraph.

[3] Blackfoot City, Montana, was a tiny mining town located, in 1865, twenty-nine miles northeast of Deer Lodge. It should not be confused with present day Blackfoot, Montana, in Glacier County, on the Great Northern Railroad. Calamity calls it Black Foot.

This story, which is of doubtful validity, states that Brown saw Calamity Jane in Confederate Gulch, Montana, not far from Blackfoot, about 1866. He judged her to be twenty or twenty-two years of age then, when she staged a one-woman stick-up in a grocery store where he was a customer. The motive for her act was to obtain food for some sick miners for whom she was caring.[4]

McClintock's narrative does much to dampen Tom Brown's story. He says that he was in Confederate Gulch shortly after 1866 where he heard the names of many who were or had been in the vicinity but recalled no mention of this gun-woman.[5]

Calamity's own account tells that, soon after her mother's death, the family moved to Utah and the father died a year later. From her statement that "we" arrived at Fort Bridger in 1868, it may be surmised that she took her brothers and sisters into Wyoming. Thereafter, no mention is made of her family, and it is probable that when she came to Wyoming she put them out of her life.

Later she went to Piedmont, Wyoming, where the Union Pacific workmen were engaged in building the railroad. There she began her life of following the construction camps. Accounts given many years later by people who saw her at that time vary as to where she was living and as to her age, though none seems to doubt her calling. In 1868 and 1869, the Union Pacific pushed through Wyoming and, to the throngs of men, this wayward girl found herself attractive. The story of what happened in Wyoming differs considerably with each narrative. One was told to McClintock by a former sheriff and deputy U. S. marshal in Deadwood, Captain John P. Belding. He claims that he knew Calamity in Cheyenne, Wyoming, in 1868 when the railroad was

[4] Tom Brown, *Romance of Everyday Life,* pp. 41-42.

[5] John S. McClintock, *Pioneer Days in the Black Hills,* p. 116.

THE YOUNG CALAMITY   Plate II

This snapshot of Calamity Jane, taken when she was about 23 years old, is one of the earliest photographs of her that can be found. It is said to have been taken in July, 1875, on Lower French Creek in the Black Hills. Reproduced through courtesy of J. Leonard Jennewein, Mitchell, S. Dak.

being built. She was known as a camp-follower and at the age of sixteen was so dissolute that she and others of her class were ordered to leave town.[6]

A different story based on circumstantial evidence appeared in the *Cheyenne Democratic Leader* in 1885. It reported that Calamity Jane came to Miners' Delight, Wyoming, in 1868 when she was eleven years old. She lived with the family of Major Gallagher. Mrs. Gallagher picked up the girl as they passed through Fort Bridger. The youngster knew nothing of her parents and was a stray from infancy. She was pretty and vivacious but in a short time her escapades shocked the whole settlement. The miners took up a collection and sent her to the railroad where for a few years she became friendly with the most degenerate railroad workers and other elements of the motley population.[7]

Paine does not think that this story can be true. He points out that reports from the local paper in Miners' Delight mentioned only Major and Mrs. Gallagher as coming to that town in 1868. Several months later James Chisholm, an eastern newspaper correspondent, visited there, some of the time as guest of the Gallaghers. In his diary he described in detail their family life but made no mention of anyone else in their home.[8]

A decided variation in the story of following the railroad construction camps is one repeated by Miguel Otero, former governor of New Mexico. He says that he saw her about Hays City, Kansas, in 1868 when she was a comparatively young woman, perhaps twenty years of age, and still extremely attractive. After a few years she left Hays City and moved from terminal town to terminal town along the advancing Kansas-Pacific

---

[6] *Ibid.,* p. 116

[7] *Cheyenne* (Wyoming) *Daily Leader,* November 3, 1885.

[8] Clarence Paine, "Calamity Jane, Man? Woman? or Both?," *Westerners Brand Book,* 1945-1946, p. 71.

Railroad, until she reached Kit Carson, Colorado. From
there she drifted to Dodge City, Granada and La Junta
along the Atchison, Topeka and Santa Fe.[9]

Two Black Hills old-timers, Jessie Brown and A. M.
Willard, perpetuate the story that Calamity was born
in Burlington, Iowa. They wrote in their book, *The
Black Hills Trails,* that she was the daughter of a Baptist minister.[10] According to their story, she ran away
from home when very young and became the mistress
of any army lieutenant. In Sidney, Nebraska, she gave
birth to a son and his father sent the infant back East
to live with his grandparents. In the meantime,
Calamity's mother married a retired soldier named Hart
and they crossed the plains to Salt Lake, Utah, picking
up the daughter along the way. Martha left her parents
in Salt Lake and went to Rawlins, Wyoming. In order
to get away, she deceived her parents, making them believe she was attending school. Later at Fort Steele,
Wyoming, she became an inmate of a bawdy house,
well-known to many soldiers and teamsters. Her mother
moved to Blackfoot, Montana, and presided over a house
of prostitution known as "Madam Canary's."[11] The latter story becomes even more colorful when Aikman
describes the mother as red-headed Madam Canary running a brothel appropriately called "The Bird Cage."[12]
Later, Brown and Willard add that Jane married a man
named White who dressed her in finery. Her life with
him soon paled, so she continued her roving, making
her headquarters around Cheyenne.[13]

Perhaps it is because there were two men working
on that "authentic history source book" that the co-
authors were able to obtain so many details about the
early life of Calamity Jane, while others working

---

[9] Miguel Otero, *My Life on the Frontier,* p. 22.

[10] They call him Reverend Canary, not Coombs, as Dr. Hendricks indicated
in his story.

[11] Jessie Brown and A. M. Willard, *The Black Hills Trails,* pp. 412-413.

[12] Duncan Aikman, *Calamity Jane and the Lady Wildcats,* pp. 42-43.

[13] Jessie Brown and A. M. Willard, p. 414.

IN FORMAL POSE   Plate III
People who knew Calamity Jane best seldom saw her dressed up as she
was when this photograph was taken. She frequently dressed as a man,
and even when she wore a skirt a gun belt or cowboy hat spoiled any
look of femininity. Photo reproduced through courtesy of A. R. McMicken,
Rawlins, Wyo.

feverishly single-handed have failed to find any authentic trace of her during these early years. However
exacting their research may have been, it is still hard
to imagine that the prim Mrs. Canary who solicitously
took care of her parishioners could be the brazen Madam
Canary who managed prostitutes.

In addition to the uncertainty and confusion which
have arisen from conflicting reports of those early years
in the life of Calamity Jane, there is the question of
her physical appearance as a young woman. So many
and so varied are the descriptions given of her at different times throughout her early life that there is certainly one to suit the taste of any interested person.
Aikman says that her hair was coppery-red,[14] while a
newspaper item from the *Nebraska Press* tells of her
sweeping raven locks.[15] A friend of Miss Estelline Bennett knew Calamity in Cheyenne as a pretty dark-eyed
girl,[16] but the *Rocky Mountain News* mentions that her
eyes "emit a greenish glare."[17] William Berry, an old
acquaintance of Calamity, said she was six feet tall,[18]
while a newspaper in 1878 called her "a little creature."[19] Otero saw her in Kansas at the age of twenty,
when she was extremely attractive.[20] Ten years later
she was described by a South Dakota paper as looking
like the "result of a cross between the gable end of a
fire proof and a Sioux Indian."[21] Miss Bennett quoted
a description of a Dr. Babcock, with whom Calamity
was supposed to have worked as a nurse in the epidemic
of 1878, to the effect that beauty was her best asset,[22]

---

[14] Aikman, p. 44.

[15] *Rocky Mountain News* (Denver, Colorado), June 10, 1877, citing *Nebraska* (Nebraska City, Nebraska) *Press.*

[16] Estelline Bennett, *Old Deadwood Days*, p. 240.

[17] *Rocky Mountain News*, January 11, 1878.

[18] Interview with Mr. William Berry August, 1949.

[19] *Rocky Mountain News*, January 11, 1878.

[20] Otero, p. 22.

[21] *Black Hills Daily Times* (Deadwood, South Dakota), September 21, 1877.

[22] Bennett. p. 222.

while a newspaper account of the same year remarked that "the old madam was not generous with her when she cast the die that moulded her."[23]

There are dozens of other statements like the ones just related which differ greatly from each other. Those who describe her all insist that they saw her at one time or another. The reason for this diversity of opinion about her appearance may be that she was such an ordinary looking person that no one noticed anything about her. If she had had an unusual or outstanding feature, all who saw her would agree almost unanimously on at least that one thing. However, since she probably had only the looks of the average frontier woman, anyone called upon to describe her might very well make up any story that seemed plausible.

Close observation of the existing pictures of her show that she had dark hair and high cheek bones. Her figure was slender as a young woman, but stocky during her later life. Shortly before her death she seemed to be slim again. In no picture is her appearance striking or even very attractive. She looks plain and mannish, in fact, whether dressed in her buckskin suit or in a dress.

It is often suggested that there are so many conflicting stories of the activities of Calamity Jane and descriptions of her person because there was more than one Calamity Jane. One view is that Martha Cannary was confused with other women who dressed in male attire. In those days few women wore trousers and the ones who did attracted attention. In January, 1877, a young female was fined ten dollars and costs in a Cheyenne, Wyoming, court for appearing on the streets in men's apparel, which implies that the number of women with whom Calamity could be confused on that score was necessarily small.

---

[23] *Daily Press and Dakotian* (Yankton, South Dakota), August 8, 1877, citing *Deadwood* (South Dakota) Champion.

There was, for example, a well-known figure in Cheyenne and surrounding towns. Her name was Minnie Watson, otherwise known as F. Frank, a worthless woman who also dressed like a man. There were rumors about her exploits with Custer which have never been proved. Her conduct and appearance may have been similar to Calamity's but there is nothing that indicates she was ever given Martha's alias. The newspapers did not confuse the two, for in January, 1877, after an item about Calamity Jane in South Dakota, the *Cheyenne Daily Leader* said that F. Frank was "still vexing the souls of the police of Laramie City."

Besides Martha Cannary, there was, however, another Calamity Jane, Mattie Young, in Denver, Colorado. From newspaper accounts it can readily be seen that she had nothing in common with Martha except her drunkenness and whoring. Since Mattie did not dress in men's clothes or roam the countryside following the soldiers, miners or cattlemen, but chose to reside safely within the city in her particular district, she could not have been easily mistaken for Calamity Jane Cannary by anyone other than local citizens. Because the accident in which the drunken Mattie Young was killed caused injury to several innocent Denver residents, the papers carried indignant reports of the wild spree in which she figured. Injured in a buggy ride while out with three other persons, the frail lady was taken to the hospital and died a few days later. Her demise came on August 26, 1878, so any confusion of the two after that date is not possible.

There may have been other women who were incorrectly called Calamity Jane, but their reputation soon died and by the time other Calamitys began to appear all over the country, Martha Cannary had so established herself that there was no longer confusion among her contemporaries.

It seems to have been the fashion, in towns where Martha Cannary had once resided or had been known, for an especially notorious woman to be named Calamity after Calamity Jane. All the residents knew that she was not *the* Calamity but they called her by that name. In Laramie an example was Mrs. Opie, alias "Kentucky Belle," alias Calamity Jane, who was sent to Fort Collins. The citizens hoped that she would keep "her ugly mug" out of town for awhile. Livingston, Montana, had a similar situation. An Annie Filmore, called Calamity Jane Number Two, was badly mauled and beaten by a male friend.[24] In Cheyenne, an infamous woman called Sarah was referred to by the local newspaper as "Calamity Sal." Found in an alley under the effects of too much alcohol, she was "toted to the cooler" by the police.[25] The three characters are typical of many others referred to by the newspapers in the 1880's. Readers today have difficulty in deciding whether the lady of whom they read was the *real* Calamity or just another local trouble-maker. It should be repeated again that the townspeople knew who their character was and seldom were confused between Cannary or Calamity Jane and the impostor.

---

[24] *Livingston* (Montana) *Enterprise,* June 12, 1886.
[25] *Cheyenne Daily Leader*, May 16, 1883.

Chapter IV.

SCOUTING

A scout was a man on the frontier whom the army used as an expert on its campaigns because of his superior knowledge of the Indians. Scouting was not necessarily an occupation. A man might be a scout on one campaign only, because he knew that particular territory and the tribes there. Usually he was a white man who refused to conform to the rules of society. Before he became a scout he roamed the prairies, mountains and deserts for years alone or in the company of the Indians. He knew thoroughly large areas of the countryside and enjoyed his wild dangerous life. Sometimes he was a full-blooded Indian or a half-breed. His main duty as a scout was to locate the Indians and ascertain their number by tracks and signs. In order to do this he ordinarily went alone in advance of the army, exposed to danger of ambush and sudden attack. He was often regarded as a brave man and sometimes even as a hero.

Calamity Jane professed to ally herself to the exalted profession of scouting at the early age of eighteen, boasting that even then she was fully able to perform the daring and difficult tasks assigned her. The beginning of her glorious life with the army she describes:

> Joined General Custer as a scout at Fort Russell, Wyoming, in 1870, and started for Arizona for the Indian Campaign. Up to this time I had always worn the costume of my sex. When I joined Custer I donned the uniform of a soldier. It was a bit awkward at first but I soon got to be perfectly at home in men's clothes.[1]

---

[1] *Autobiography*, p. 2.

The trousers and paraphernalia of a soldier may have been "a bit awkward at first" but still more awkward for the story is the fact that Custer never was at Fort D. A. Russell. He never in his lifetime set foot inside the bounds of Arizona, much less fought in the Indian campaigns there. By a careful check of Custer's every move it is easy to deduct where he was not.[2] In 1870, while Calamity maintained she was scouting with him, he was at Fort Leavenworth, Kansas writing his *War Memoirs.* He even obtained leave and with his wife visited New York. In the summer of 1870 he went on hunting expeditions with tourists attracted west by his fame.[3]

Another military assignment from her *Life and Adventures* goes:

> We were afterwards ordered to Fort Custer, where Custer city now stands, where we arrived in the spring of 1874; remained around Fort Custer all summer and were ordered to Fort Russell in fall of 1874, where we remained until spring of 1875.[4]

Since Fort Custer was not built until 1878 it is hard to imagine just how or why Calamity was ordered there in the spring of 1874 to remain until that fall.[5] (Editor's note: There is some possibility that Calamity's reference to Fort Custer may be to a very temporary camp which General Custer used during his Black Hills expedition.)

Calamity Jane claimed that in 1875 she went with the troops when they were ordered to the Black Hills. There is some indication that she went in that year in some capacity or other with the Jenney Expedition. Here is what she says of the trip:

> was then ordered to the Black Hills to protect miners, as that country was controlled by the Sioux In-

---

[2] Frederic F. Van de Water, *Glory Hunter* and Frederick Whittaker, *A Complete Life of General George A. Custer.*
[3] *Ibid.,* pp. 473-476.
[4] *Autobiography,* p. 3.
[5] Edgar M. Ledyard, "American Posts," *Utah Historical Quarterly,* October, 1928, p. 122.

AS A "SCOUT"   Plate IV

This picture of Calamity Jane dressed in buckskin and holding a Stevens buggy gun, is, like the picture in Plate V, frequently used to further the belief that she was a scout for General Crook and others. Said to have been taken in about 1876, this picture was found under an old building and since its resurrection has adorned hundreds of tourist postcards. Historical Society of Montana photo.

dians and the government had to send the soldiers to protect the lives of the miners and settlers in that section. Remained there until fall of 1875 and wintered in Fort Laramie.[6]

By the treaty of April, 1868, the Sioux Indians were given an immense reservation of which the Black Hills were part. In 1874 Custer made a hasty trip through that country to obtain information for the government about the region. The several miners with the expedition found gold distributed in gulches throughout the area. The news of gold, though only modest mention was made of it by the miners and Custer, fired the imagination of American prospectors and frontiersmen. Many wanted badly to go to the new fields but expressed no wish to transgress the word of the government given in the treaty to stay off the reservation. They thought the government should either buy the Black Hills or get some concession from the Indians. So the Secretary of Interior appointed several trustworthy persons to examine the region for paying quantities of gold. The facts learned about the mineral deposits would give a basis for subsequent negotiations with Indians for the territory.

Walter P. Jenney was commissioned to undertake this work. Henry Newton was to act as assistant while V. T. McGillycuddy, M.D., late of the Lake and Northern Boundary Surveys, was appointed topographer. Thirteen other men ranging from astronomer to cook made up the civilian personnel. As military escort there were four hundred men with a train of seventy-five wagons under Lieutenant Colonel R. I. Dodge. The two groups assembled near Fort Laramie May 24, 1875, and began the journey which covered the entire area of the Black Hills between the forks of the Cheyenne. On October 14, 1875, the expedition returned to Fort Laramie, having met no Indians during the five months

[6] *Autobiography,* p. 3.

in the field.[7] It was with this group that Calamity is supposed to have made her first trip into the Black Hills.

Dr. McGillycuddy, the topographer, has related a rather long circumstantial story of Calamity Jane's part in this expedition. He always insisted that she made the entire trip. He later remembered that, according to her, Colonel Dodge had refused her permission to go. She then had appealed to the topographer to put in a good word for her, but he had explained it would be useless since he had nothing to do with the personnel assigned to the party. Calamity was determined, for her then current lover, a Sergeant Shaw, was a trooper in the cavalry detailed to Colonel Dodge's assignment. Dressed like a trooper she went with the expedition.

Four days out from Laramie, Calamity Jane was discovered when striding from the soldiers' section past the officers' quarters to the sutler's store at the other end of camp. Unfortunately, she met the officer of the day to whom she rendered a snappy salute. He acknowledged it and passed on, only to find several soldiers snickering at him. He demanded to know the cause of their merriment and was told that he had just met and saluted Calamity Jane. The incident was reported to Dodge who knew that he must get rid of her. It seemed heartless to send her back sixty miles through the wilderness to Fort Laramie. But discipline had to be maintained and he ordered her to go. As the expedition pulled out the next morning Calamity, standing with her pony by the trail, watched the troops pass by her. She was not worried, however. As the wagon train and train guard brought up the rear, she turned her pony in among the led horses, slipped under a

[7] U. S. Geographical and Geological Survey of the Rocky Mountain Region, *Report on the Geology and Resources of the Black Hills of Dakota, with Atlas* by Henry Newton and Walter P. Jenney, pp. 15-21.

wagon bow and disappeared from sight. The next day she was discovered and ordered away again. The ceremony was repeated daily during the whole trip.[8]

A more revealing story about the discovery of Calamity in Dodge's army has its coterie of followers, even though its origin is still more doubtful than the other. It is probably but another of the exaggerated accounts of Holbrook:

> While the Jenney party was being formed and equipped at Fort Laramie, one of its enlisted men, Sergeant Frank Siechrist, met up with Calamity Jane . . . and got her rigged up in the baggy, shapeless clothes of the enlisted man of 1875, and away she went to the Black Hills . . . At some stop along the way, after the party had camped one evening, an officer strolling near a stream to watch the soldiers swimming was struck dumb—we can presume—for Jane was right in there with the boys and she had troubled herself no more than they about a bathing suit. She was promptly sent back to Fort Laramie.[9]

Evidence supporting neither of these stories is conclusive, and indeed there is no absolute proof that she made the trip at all, even as a camp-follower.

Before the Jenney Expedition returned to its base, the Government began negotiations for buying the Black Hills, but failed to reach an agreement with the Indians.[10] Apprehensive of what was to follow, the army began to strengthen its power around the Sioux reservation and the unceded territory of the Sioux. General George Crook was in command of the Department of the Platte with headquarters at Fort Fetterman. In March, 1876, Crook was instructed to reduce the Indians to subjugation.[11] There is positive evidence that

[8] Julia B. McGillycuddy, *McGillycuddy Agent*, pp. 30-34.
[9] Stewart H. Holbrook, *Little Annie Oakley and Other Rugged People*, pp. 32-33.
[10] Charles Deland, *The Sioux Wars*, p. 212.
[11] *Ibid.*, p. 220.

Calamity Jane was with the troops on this expedition. Just exactly what she was doing and how long she remained with the outfit is a point for speculation. On February 21, 1876, I. N. Bard[12] wrote in his diary:

> Very pleasant all day. Left town at 9 a. m. Made a short call at Pole Creek. There is six or eight Black Hills teams here. Drove over to Fagans. He is crowded full. Calamity Jane is here going up with the troops. I think there is trouble ahead. Everything is crowded here. There is seven Companies on the road.[13]

When Crook's expedition returned without accomplishing anything, General Sheridan ordered three separate columns to advance into southeastern Montana near the Big Horn region. The first column was under General John Gibbon and consisted of troops from the Montana camps; the second under General Alfred Terry started from Fort Lincoln, Dakota; the third column was under General Crook.[14] The latter was to move from Fort Fetterman along the same route that he had taken in March, past Camp Reno and Fort Kearney into Big Horn country and eventually unite with the two other strong columns. Under Terry was Custer with his Seventh Cavalry.

In command of fifteen companies of cavalry and five companies of infantry, General Crook moved out from Fetterman on May 29, 1876, heading northwest. Three days later a heavy snow storm made the day miserable and drove the temperature so low that the water froze in the camp kettles. On June 9, the monotony of camp life was broken by an attack of Sioux and Cheyennes.[15] Some time after that attack and before

---

[12] Bard worked for John (Portugee) Phillips at Chugwater, Wyoming. Later he owned Bard's Ranch on the Little Bear. The "town" referred to is Cheyenne.

[13] This unpublished diary is in the Agnes Wright Spring Collection, Western History Department, Denver Public Library, Denver, Colorado.

[14] John Gregory Bourke, *"On the Border with Crook,* p. 285.

[15] *Ibid.,* pp. 289-296.

PUBLICITY POSE   Plate V

Complete with cartridge belt and rifle, Calamity Jane posed here as a scout
for General Crook. Research fails to credit her with being a regularly
employed scout or guide. This was strictly a publicity pose and tourists
have bought copies of it by the hundreds. Historical Society of Montana
photo.

June 14, Lieutenant Bourke, aide-de-camp for Crook, noted in his diary that it was whispered one of their teamsters was Calamity Jane. Her sex was discovered when the wagon-master noted that she did not cuss her mules with the enthusiasm to be expected from a graduate of Patrick and Saulsbury's Black Hills Stage Line, as she had represented herself to be.[16] In corroboration with the lieutenant on that point was Captain Anson Mills, well-known soldier under Crook, who said he saw and talked to her during that same campaign. His explanation was that, in organizing the wagon train, the wagon-master had inadvertently hired Calamity who was not discovered until the outfit neared Fort Reno. After her arrest she was placed in improvised female attire and carried along until a force was organized to carry back the wounded, with whom she was sent.[17] Both accounts seem logical enough and might be accepted if it were not for a Cheyenne newspaper item at that time:

> On Sunday, June 10 that notorious female, Calamity Jane greatly rejoiced over her release from durance vile, procured a horse and buggy from Jas. Abney's stable, ostensibly to drive to Fort Russell and back. By the time she had reached the Fort, however, indulgence in frequent and liberal potations completely befogged her not very clear brain, and she drove right by that place never drawing rein until she reached the Chug fifty miles distant. Continuing to imbibe bug-juice at close intervals and in large quantities throughout the night, she woke up the next morning with a vague idea that Fort Russell had been moved but being still bent on finding it, she drove on, finally sighting Fort Laramie, ninety miles distant. Reaching there she discovered her mistake, but didn't show much disappointment. She turned her horse out to grass, ran

---

[16] *Ibid.*, pp. 299-300.
[17] Anson Mills, *My Story*, p. 397.

the buggy into a corral, and began enjoying life in camp after her usual fashion. When Joe Rankin reached the Fort, several days later, she begged him not to arrest her, and as he had no authority to do so, he merely took charge of Abney's outfit which was brought back to this city Sunday.[18]

Lieutenant Bourke did not say that he had actually seen Calamity or knew her presence to be a fact, but only that "it was whispered that one of our teamsters was a woman, and no other than 'Calamity Jane.' "[19] Captain Mills, however, related a comical incident on the trip in which he was personally involved with her. His story was that the day she was discovered and placed under guard, he was going through the wagon-master's outfit. As he passed, Calamity Jane called out, "There is Colonel Mills, he knows me!" It turned out that she had often seen Mills in the home of a friend where Calamity had been hired as a cook. He was much chagrined at such familiarity from a woman of her class and turned away. This story Mills told when reminiscing about the Rosebud Expedition in an address before the Order of Indian Wars in 1917, forty years after the campaign.[20] Without questioning his ability as an army officer, or integrity as a person, it is easy to imagine that he threw in the fanciful tale of Calamity Jane to liven up a somewhat gloomy subject.

Calamity's own story of her work with Crook has afforded much material for fiction writers and historians:

> In spring of 1876, we were ordered north with General Crook to join Gen'ls Miles, Terry and Custer at Big Horn river. During this march I swam the Platte river at Fort Fetterman as I was the bearer of important dispatches. I had a ninety mile ride to

[18] *Cheyenne* (Wyoming) *Daily Leader*, June 20, 1876.
[19] Bourke, pp. 299-300.
[20] Mills, p. 397.

GENERAL GEORGE CUSTER   Plate VI

In her Autobiography, Calamity Jane said she joined General Custer's
troops at Fort Russell, Wyoming, in 1870. Custer was never at Fort Russell, however, and at the time Calamity said she was scouting for him, the
ill-fated Custer was writing his war memoirs at Fort Leavenworth, Kansas. Historical Society of Montana photo.

make, being wet and cold, I contracted a severe illness and was sent back in Gen. Crook's ambulance to Fort Fetterman where I laid in the hospital for fourteen days.[21]

It is comparatively easy to point out how palpably incorrect are the statements "by herself." A few of the following errors plus the above newspaper quotation show without doubt that Calamity Jane had no part in the Battle of the Rosebud. It was General Gibbon, not Miles, whom Crook was to join. If Jane had been scouting, certainly she would have known exactly whom she might expect to meet when the forces united, even though recalling the battle twenty years later. Furthermore, the scouts were named by Lieutenant Bourke as Frank Gruard, "to whom the whole country was as familiar as a book," Louis Richaud and Baptiste "Big Bat" Pourrier.[22] Just when she was required to carry dispatches back to Fort Fetterman is hard to visualize, as only one return trip was made before the wounded were sent back. A courier named Harrison undertook the dangerous job of carrying official communications back to Fetterman.[23] This fort was on the north side of the Platte, which meant that no one need cross the Platte to get from Crook to the fort. There were no written dispatches between Crook and Gibbon, because the Crow Indians supplied the news. Up until the end of June, no word was received from General Terry and his command.[24] Where, then, was she delivering all of her important messages? The ninety-mile ride about which she wrote might have been, in reality, the wild goose chase she made from Cheyenne to Fort Laramie mentioned in the newspaper. If she had been a teamster on the Rosebud Expedition with Crook, which she obviously was not, she no doubt would have ridden back

---

[21] *Autobiography*, p. 4.
[22] Bourke, p. 290.
[23] *Ibid.*, p. 298.
[24] *Ibid.*, p. 301.

in a wagon or ambulance for the wounded, but under guard and not because she contracted an illness requiring two weeks' hospitalization.

Writers have been prone to combine bits of Calamity's story with pieces of the newspaper item and come out with exciting new stories. Typical of many historic attempts to show the true Calamity Jane is the one by Miss Estelline Bennett:

> She came into the Black Hills first with General Crook's command in the summer of '75 when he had marched in from Fort Laramie to order the miners out of the Hills until treaties could be made with the Indians. Calamity had been in Cheyenne getting a little bored and restless when she heard of the proposed expedition into a new, wild, and dangerous country. The day she heard about it, she hired a team and buggy to "go for a little ride," she told the man at the livery stable. She drove her horses at an easy trot through the streets of Cheyenne, but when she had left the city behind she speeded up and drove as rapidly as her consideration for horses would permit. Arrived at Fort Laramie, she left her rig where its owner could recover it, smuggled herself in among the soldiers, and was too far on the way to the outlaw country to be sent back, before anyone discovered she was a woman.[25]

Deadwood merchants today are making easy money from gullible Black Hills tourists who buy postcards like the two shown in Plates IV and V. When, after much research, it is difficult to prove that Calamity Jane ever accompanied the troops even as a bullwhacker, such statements as those on the postcards, exalting her as a scout, are ridiculous.

[25] Estelline Bennett, *Old Deadwood Days,* p. 233.

FORT CUSTER   Plate VII

This southeastern Montana fort was one of several army posts that Calamity Jane frequented. She says in her Autobiography that she and the troops were ordered here in the Spring of 1874. Since this fort was not built until 1878, her facts are of course incorrect. This picture shows the officers' quarters and parade ground. Historical Society of Montana photo.

FORT FETTERMAN   Plate IX

The expedition under General Crook to subdue the Sioux left from this Wyoming fort in March, 1876. This was one adventure in which Calamity Jane, dressed in men's clothing, apparently had a part. It is believed possible that she was also in the earlier Jenney Expedition into the Black Hills. Historical Society of Montana photo.

GENERAL GEORGE CROOK   Plate VIII

General Crook, commander of the Department of the Platte with headquarters at Fort Fetterman, was instructed in March of 1876 to reduce the
Sioux to subjugation after negotiations with them for the Black Hills had
failed. There is evidence that Calamity Jane was with this expedition.
South Dakota Historical Society photo.

Chapter V.

NICKNAME

The origin of the nickname, Calamity Jane, has been dealt with by every old-timer, historian, journalist, montebank and poor man's philosopher who has felt called upon to comment on this woman of the frontier. A few agree with George Hoshier, an old friend and pall-bearer at Calamity Jane's funeral, that she had the name early in life because she was prone to Calamity. In the colorful words of that old pioneer, "if she sat on a fence rail it would rare up and buck her off."[1] Another account states that she got the name after her outstanding service in Deadwood's smallpox epidemic of 1878[2] but by that time she had already been Calamity Jane for several years. The *St. Paul Dispatch* of July 13, 1901, explained it as follows: "She gets her name from a faculty she has had of producing a ruction at any time and place and on short notice." Dr. V. T. McGillycuddy stated that she was called Calamity because of the calamitous deaths of her father and mother.[3] Since the topographer has been shown to be a writer of doubtful reliability, this theory can also be questioned.

Perhaps the earliest and most imaginative account of the captious appellation appeared in a highly fictionalized story, "Calamity Jane, Queen of the Plains." In that sensational tale, Jesse James inquired about her doleful sobriquet. Her gloomy reply to that frontier bad man is as follows:

---

[1] *Great Falls* (Montana) *Leader*, July 16, 1906.

[2] Lewis Crawford, *Rekindling Camp Fires*, p. 274.

[3] Dr. V. T. McGillycuddy to Editor of the *Rapid City Journal*, October 1, 1924, South Dakota Historical Society Library.

When I went to a mining town in Colorado at first, I was simply known as Jane—by some called 'Pretty Jane.' But wherever I went some great evil came upon some of the men or their families . . . Their wives would fall into old shafts and break their necks, some of the men would accidentally shoot themselves, or so it was supposed, when a man was found with a barrel of his own pistol empty and he dead beside it on the ground. Children belonging to such men got lost, and weren't found till they had starved to death in some lone gulch. And as wherever I moved these things happened, people began to think I had the 'evil eye' and carried bad luck wtih me, and they called me Calamity Jane. I've borne the ominous name for years.[4]

In addition to scores of suggestions like the ones mentioned, there are two main versions, each of which has numerous adherents. The first theory appeared in Calamity's *Autobiography*, which was not published till 1896. Calamity may have been giving the same thrilling story long before that to a generation of "bar-flies" and "greenhorns." She may just once have been cajoled by the hoax-lovers into reenacting the scene for a crowd of "tenderfeet," and been stuck with the story. Estelline Bennett's uncle, General Dawson, stated once that Calamity Jane in her later days had lost track of which stories were true and which were not.[5] Here is Calamity's story, as told in the pamphlet:

After that campaign I returned to Fort Sanders, Wyoming, remained there until spring of 1872, when we were ordered out to the Muscle Shell or Nursey Pursey Indian outbreak. In the war Generals Custer, Miles, Terry and Crook were all engaged. This campaign lasted until fall of 1873. It was during this

---

[4] Reckless Ralph, "Calamity Jane, Queen of the Plains," *Street and Smith's New York Weekly,* January 23, 1882. p. 3.
[5] Estelline Bennett, *Old Deadwood Days,* p. 234.

GENERAL JOHN GIBBON   Plate X

When Crook's expedition returned without accomplishing its purpose of
successfully engaging the Sioux, General Sheridan sent out three separate
columns to advance into southeastern Montana, the first column being under
General Gibbon, pictured here. Historical Society of Montana photo.

campaign that I was christened Calamity Jane. It was on Goose Creek, Wyoming, where the town of Sheridan is now located. Capt. Egan was in command of the Post. We were ordered out to quell an uprising of the Indians, and were out for several days, had numerous skirmishes during which six of the soldiers were killed and several severely wounded. When on returning to the Post we were ambushed about a mile and a half from our destination. When fired upon Capt. Egan was shot. I was riding in advance and on hearing the firing turned in my saddle and saw the Captain reeling in his saddle as though about to fall. I turned my horse and galloped back with all haste to his side and got there in time to catch him as he was falling. I lifted him onto my horse in front of me and succeeded in getting him safely to the Fort. Capt. Egan on recovering, laughingly said: "I name you Calamity Jane, the heroine of the plains." I have borne that name up to the present time.[6]

This exciting quotation can be proved to contain little truth. The only accurate statement is that Sheridan, Wyoming, is near Goose Creek.

One historian has an informative sidelight about the "rescuer" and the "rescued." He wrote that "her only traceable relation with Egan was when she laundered his uniform, while he remembered that he ordered her and another woman off the reservation because of their bad influence on the men."[7] Captain Jack Crawford, one time chief of scouts in the United States Army, refuted the Egan theory when he said that he "was with Captain Egan and his White Horse troop and helped patrol the roads between Fort Laramie and Red Canyon, and no such fight ever took place, nor was Captain Egan

---

[6] *Autobiography*, p. 3.

[7] Harold E. Briggs, *Frontiers of the Northwest*, p. 80.

wounded."[8] Egan was a colorful personality and the kind of man with whom Calamity would have liked to be permanently linked.

In 1872 and 1873, the Nez Perce Indians were stolid and placid, roaming around at home in Idaho. Those were not war years but revival years when missionaries were busy preaching to their people and baptizing them at a near record rate.[9] The Nez Perce War lasted from June, 1877, until October of the same year. That brave trek would scarcely be called either an uprising or outbreak by a soldier or scout familiar with the war. Besides, Calamity was not there when the actual fighting took place. During July, August and September of the five-month campaign she was conspicuously seen in three different states far away from either the fleeing Indians or pursuing army. When she showed up in Wyoming the first week in July the paper noted: "The return of the well-known frontierswoman, Calamity Jane, to Cheyenne, which took place yesterday, was one of the few events of a dull sultry July day."[10] August 4, she appeared in Sidney, Nebraska. The *Sidney Telegraph* reported: "Calamity Jane has arrived from the Black Hills. She received promotion on the road as assistant wagon boss." In true character, a month later she gave Deadwood, South Dakota, newspaper men an excellent chance to display their journalistic talents:

> That 'heroine of the Hills,' who figured so largely in the local columns of our contemporary this morning, didn't 'pan out' very well upon investigation. She is a low down prostitute who has been herding with Indians, negroes, and soldiers, for the past year . . . Instead of leaving town on a high mettled steed, as described by the romantic local of the *Pioneer*, she repaired to Chinatown and got drunk.

[8] *Rapid City* (South Dakota) *Journal*, no date on clipping in files South Dakota Historical Society Library. Context tells that it must have been a few weeks after Calamity Jane's death, August 1, 1903.

[9] Kate C. McBeth, *The Nez Perces Since Lewis and Clark*, pp. 73-83.

[10] *Cheyenne* (Wyoming) *Sun*, July 7, 1877.

GENERAL NELSON MILES   Plate XI

Calamity Jane said in her own story that she was active in the Nez Perce
Indian outbreak in which General Miles, among others, was engaged. The
record shows, however, that she was far away from the scene. Her claims
of vital duty for the commanders during the Indian wars have not been
proven true. Historical Society of Montana photo.

She was met there last evening with a bloody nose, and, upon being asked where she was going, answered, 'God knows, I don't.' That is the kind of a heroine she is.[11]

Generals Howard and Gibbon and Colonels Sturgis and Miles were the leaders in the attack on the Indians, not Generals Custer, Terry and Crook as stated by Calamity Jane. Custer, for example was not encountering Indians in 1872 and 1873 and, during the time that the Nez Perce fighting was going on in 1877, he had been dead for one year. Likewise, Crook had nothing to do with the Nez Perces. From 1871 through 1875 he dealt with the fierce Apaches in Arizona and, during Chief Joseph's retreat, he was busy trying to put the Sioux agencies into respectable shape. There are similar time discrepancies for Terry and Miles in 1872-1873 so it can be concluded that she did not know who was in charge of the Nez Perce War.

Chief Joseph did not lead his people nearly so far east as to the post where Calamity Jane claimed she was stationed. From Yellowstone Park in western Wyoming the Indians went nearly due north into Montana, while Calamity was in central Wyoming on the eastern side of the Big Horn Mountains. So many errors in geographical location, dates, wars and military leaders show that the Goose Creek incident could not possibly have taken place, and since it did not, the inception of the name Calamity Jane could not have occurred in the way the *Autobiography* states.

Next in popularity to her own story involving Captain Egan comes the more logical but unfounded story which had its earliest appearance in the obituary notice for Calamity Jane. The Deadwood paper suggested that "the name is said to have been applied to her by Bill Nye during the early seventies when he was editing

---

[11] *Black Hills Daily Times* (Deadwood, South Dakota), September 21, 1877.

the *Laramie Boomerang*."[12] Before the validity of that statement can be analyzed, the reader must know that Calamity received her nickname before February, 1876. The first contemporary mention of her as Calamity Jane was February 21, 1876, when I. N. Bard wrote in his diary: "Calamity Jane is here going up with the troops."[13] The *Laramie Boomerang* was founded in 1881, at least five years after she became Calamity. Bill Nye came from Wisconsin to Wyoming in the late spring of 1876 and began his western newspaper career on the *Laramie Daily Sentinel* sometime after May 10.[14] Three months previously, Mr. Bard saw Martha Cannary whom he referred to as Calamity Jane. It is, however, possible that the great humorist, Nye, did at one time suggest that Calamity Jane was so named because "hard luck and Martha Cannary always went hand in hand,"[15] but under no circumstance could he have done the original naming in either the *Sentinel* or *Boomerang*.

Perhaps Martha Cannary was not named Calamity Jane because of any one particular episode such as the Goose Creek incident or by any person as respected as Bill Nye. In the early days even the most casual observer of that lewd "jane-about-town" must have noticed that activity seemed to spring up wherever she was, and conversely, that she followed excitement wherever it went. So, it is possible that Martha could have become Calamity Jane by the slightest accident.

---

[12] *Pioneer-Times* (Deadwood, South Dakota), August 2, 1903. This writer became enthusiastic over the *Laramie Boomerang* suggestion and boarded a bus for Cheyenne. At the Wyoming State Historical Library she hoped to find the Bill Nye quotation among the early 1870 Boomerangs. Undaunted, after a long hot trip, by the fact that the library had no early Laramie papers whatsoever, she put in a call to the University Library in Laramie to make sure it had the desired papers before making another journey. While waiting for the call to go through, the author discovered a pertinent book, *The Life of Bill Nye,* lying on the shelf, glanced through it and found that Bill Nye's *Boomerang* was not founded until 1881, more than five years too late to be of value for this study.

[13] This unpublished diary is in the Agnes Wright Spring Collection, Western History Department, Denver Public Library, Denver, Colorado.

[14] Reference Librarian, University of Wyoming, to Roberta Sollid, June 21, 1950, in the files of this author.

[15] Frank J. Wilstach, *Wild Bill Hickok,* p. 262.

Calamity Jane never did say that any part of her real name included "Jane." In the first sentence of the *Autobiography* she stated: "My maiden name was Martha Cannary . . ." When she was buried in Deadwood her tombstone was marked Mrs. M. E. Burke. Her husband's name was Clinton Burke so there was no confusion of initials between Calamity and Mr. Burke. Since Jane, the second word of the nickname, was so important in Calamity's career, why did she not mention her maiden name as Martha *Jane* Cannary? Deadwood residents knew her as Calamity Jane for years and yet they buried her not M. J. but M. E. Burke. The answer might be that Jane was not her middle name and that whatever her middle name was, it began with an E. Today, especially in society on Calamity's level, a young woman is often called a skirt, a twist, a femme, or by an old expression, a jane. That latter title might well have been used by many in the middle 1870's when referring to Calamity. How easy for someone talking about the escapades of Martha E. Cannary to have said, "Calamity sure follows that jane and I guess from all I hear that jane follows calamity. Maybe we ought to call her Calamity Jane." From some such statement the epithet could have taken hold and stuck. In an age of Madame Moustache, Kitty the Schemer, Deadwood Dick, and Wild Bill Hickok, a name like Calamity Jane would have had no trouble immediately becoming part of the frontier vocabulary.

"ONLY AND ORIGINAL" CALAMITY   Plate XII

"Only and Original Calamity Jane" is the title given this portrait taken in
1880 by the late L. A. Huffman, the early-day photographer who left one
of Montana's most complete photographic records. This formal pose is reproduced through the courtesy of the photographer's daughter, Mrs. Ruth
Huffman Scott of Miles City.

Chapter VI.

HUSBANDS, LAWFUL and CASUAL

The name of Wild Bill Hickok has often been intimately linked with that of Calamity Jane in both the movies and dime novels. Most historians, however, are reticent about agreeing that there was a marriage or even a romance between the two. The writers to whom Wild Bill is a hero will argue that he was too fastidious to have anything to do with such a woman.

On her deathbed, Calamity Jane muttered something about being buried next to Wild Bill but this was probably one of her fantastic ideas. During her active life, as far as is known, she said little that would indicate any special affection for him. In 1902 when asked by a noted explorer about the truth of the story, "Jane of the Plains," which had tender love scenes between Calamity and Bill, she said that the "thriller" was full of "blankety-blank lies."[1] Her *Autobiography* makes only brief mention of him: "I started for Fort Laramie were I met Wm. Hickok better known as Wild Bill, and we started for Deadwood, where we arrived about June."[2]

There is some question about when the two arrived in Deadwood, but most authorities have settled upon sometime in June, 1876. Since most of the newspaper files of that town were destroyed by fire in 1879 and the rest stolen, exact information is hard to obtain. Despite that fact, the date of their arrival can be narrowed down to between June 15 and July 15, 1876. An outside source, the *Cheyenne Daily Leader* of July 30 carried a four-word news item from the *Black Hills Pioneer* of July 15, which said, "Calamity Jane has arrived." It has already been noted that she was at Fort Laramie about June 15.[3] This fact is in line with her own state-

[1] Lewis Freeman, *Down the Yellowstone,* p. 76.
[2] *Autobiography,* p. 4.
[3] *Cheyenne* (Wyoming) *Daily Leader,* June 20, 1876.

41

ment that she met Wild Bill at Fort Laramie and they reached Deadwood in June. Captain Jack Crawford, the poet scout, said that he talked to Bill sometime that June in Cheyenne and Bill told him that up to that time he had never seen Calamity Jane.[4] Since Fort Laramie was ninety miles north of Cheyenne and on the direct route to Deadwood, it is reasonable to assume that Wild Bill did meet Calamity there or at some other point along the way in late June and that the two journeyed together to Deadwood the latter part of that month or early in July.

McClintock wrote that he saw the party come into Deadwood probably sometime in the month of June, 1876. It consisted of Calamity Jane, Wild Bill Hickok, Kittie Arnold, Colorado Charlie Utter and his brother, Steve. Calamity was dressed in a new, elegant well-fitted man's suit of buckskin and was encompassed by a belt of "arsenals." For the short time that Wild Bill remained alive after this, Calamity was seen frequently in his company usually following him about the streets[5] "as a dog follows its master."[6]

Another on-the-spot witness to the spectacular entry of the little party was Mr. Richard B. Hughes, first editor of the *Rapid City Journal.* He recalled that the troupe came into Deadwood and rode the entire length of Main Street, mounted on good horses and clad completely in buckskin, every suit of which carried enough fringe to make a considerable buckskin rope. Calamity,

---

[4] *Rapid City* (South Dakota) *Journal,* no date on clipping which is on file at the South Dakota Historical Society Library. Context tells that it must have been a few weeks after Calamity Jane's death, August 1, 1903.

[5] John S. McClintock, *Pioneer Days in the Black Hills,* p. 117.

According to E. L. Senn, editor of McClintock's book, the author knew Wild Bill in Missouri before they both migrated to Deadwood. McClintock had been a sympathizer of the South during the Civil War and Wild Bill a Union soldier. The former did not like Hickok but when the latter came to Deadwood he asked permission to pitch his tent on McClintock's property and was given permission. Senn said McClintock was always very just and honest in his criticism of Bill and reserved his personal feelings for himself.

[6] Mr. Senn quoted McClintock as having often said that phrase, "as a dog follows its master," although McClintock did not add it in his book.

WILD BILL HICKOK   Plate XIII
Calamity Jane's connection with Wild Bill Hickok has been one of the
most eagerly romanticized aspects of her life. The one thing certain is
that she wanted to be buried next to him in Deadwood, and this request
was carried out. Whether he would have approved such an arrangement
is questioned by historians, and especially by Hickok's admirers. Historical
Society of Montana photo.

IN ELEGANT LEATHER SUIT   Plate XIV

Calamity Jane was dressed in an "elegant well-fitted men's suit of buck-skin" much like she is wearing here when she came to Deadwood in the Summer of 1876 with a party which included Wild Bill Hickok. This picture was taken in Evanston, Wyo., and is from the Jack Ledbetter Collection. University of Wyoming Library photo.

riding astride, attracted considerable attention, though for all her notoriety she was basking chiefly in the reflected glory of Wild Bill.[7]

Frank Wilstach, probably the most widely quoted biographer of Wild Bill, objects to any insinuation that Calamity was a paramour of Bill. In his book, published in 1926, he protested about a letter written for the Deadwood *Pioneer-Times* in 1923 by McClintock, who said that "Hickok drifted, in the month of June, into Deadwood, accompanied by his consort, Calamity Jane."[8] In 1939, when McClintock published his own book, he answered Wilstach and others who had challenged him as follows:

> In a former story by this writer of some occurrences of those days, the statement was made that Wild Bill was frequently seen while in Deadwood, walking on the streets with two six-shooters stuck under the waist band of his pants, with no scabbards in sight, and that he was being followed by his "consort", Calamity Jane. The latter part of this statement has been disputed by some of his admirers. They contend that Wild Bill would not so lower himself, and that "Colorado Charlie" was her man. Nevertheless, it is a fact that she came to Deadwood with him and others, followed him up and down the streets, accompanied him to and from the restaurants, and after he was killed, wailed over his body and invoked maledictions upon the head of the murderer.[9]

---

[7] *Memoirs of Richard B. Hughes,* pp. 143-144. (unpublished).

Duncan Aikman used Mr. Hughes' book as source material for this particular part of the story. From one page of the original, Aikman developed about fifteen pages in his own story. His account is extremely colorful and frequently quoted.

[8] Frank J. Wilstach, *Wild Bill Hickok*, p. 254.

McClintock's letter of January 10, 1923, does not appear in the *Pioneer-Times* under that date, nor in any of the papers a few weeks before or after it. There is probably a typographical error in the date. Over a period of ten or fifteen years McClintock wrote a number of letters, usually pertaining to the days of '76, which were published in the *Pioneer-Times.*

[9] John S. McClintock, p. 106.

Wild Bill was assassinated August 2, 1876, at the Nuttall and Mann saloon (also called Saloon No. 10) while playing a game of poker. McClintock added that after Bill's death Calamity "never appeared to show any preference for any particular one of the numerous element who depended upon the resources of one of her class for the price of a cigar, a drink, a meal, or a stake at 'Bank the Wheel.' "[10]

A recent development in the Calamity Jane-Wild Bill romance came in 1941 when Mrs. Jane Hickok McCormick was interviewed on Mother's Day by Gabriel Heater. Mrs. McCormick announced to the world that her own mother was Calamity Jane and her father Wild Bill.[11] With a diary and various papers to offer as evidence, Mrs. McCormick, until her death in February, 1951, made a valiant effort to prove the authenticity of those documents.[12] The marriage statement, which is supposed to record the marriage of Calamity and Bill on their way to Abilene, Kansas, in September, 1870, is written on a page in a Bible. Signatures of witnesses, Calamity's signature and Bill's are carefully done in different script. Wild Bill's age is given as thirty-one. That does not correspond to the date given by his several biographers, who place his birth date as 1837, which made him thirty-three at the time of his marriage. Calamity's age is recorded as eighteen, which is in accordance with her own version that she was born in 1852. Paine claimed that this paper can be proved to be a forgery, but gave no details.[13] The motive for such a forgery could easily be found in Mrs. McCormick's wish to legitimatize her descent or receive publicity which could be turned into remunerative channels.

---

[10] *Ibid.*, p. 118.

[11] *Buffalo* (Wyoming) *Bulletin*, May 17, 1941.

[12] The present writer has a photostatic copy of the marriage statement and numerous pages from the diary.

[13] Clarence Paine, "She Laid Her Pistol Down," *Westerners Brand Book*, 1944, p. 15.

In letters and over the National Broadcasting Company network, Jane Hickok claimed that she was born at Benson's Landing, near the site of present Livingston, Montana, in September, 1873. Here is a part of a letter she wrote when applying for a position in Virginia City, Montana, on the occasion of its revival as a pioneer town:

> Of course, Calamity Jane had left Wild Bill early that year (1873). She had been posing as his partner, the Jack of Diamonds, in Abilene, Kansas, and down on the Border. She left him in Deadwood and hit the trail alone up the Yellowstone Valley. She was only nineteen when I was born. She had no care of any sort and almost died from lack of medical care.[14]

One glaring inaccuracy is that Calamity could not have left Wild Bill in Deadwood in 1873, as there was no such town at that early date. In fact, the Black Hills had not yet been thoroughly explored by white men. A second obvious error is that if Calamity had been eighteen at the time of her marriage as shown on the statement in 1870, she would have been twenty-one when her child was born at Benson's Landing, not nineteen as the daughter claimed. Because there are no facts to prove what either Calamity or Wild Bill was doing between 1870 and 1873, no real denial can be made to Mrs. McCormick's tale. However, her stories are so out of line with other known facts that they can be dismissed. For example, in the late 1880's newspapers were referring to Calamity as "a wreck of what might once have been a woman" and similar phrases;[15] yet the daughter recalled that Calamity took an ocean voyage in the 1890's, and, dressed in a beautiful black velvet dress, was the "belle of the ball."[16]

---

[14] Mrs. Jane Hickok-McCormick to Mr. Charles Bovey, June 23, 1947, Montana Historical Society Library.

[15] *Laramie* (Wyoming) *Boomerang*, February 28, 1887.

[16] *Buffalo Bulletin*, May 17, 1941.

If the *Cheyenne Daily Leader* of January 26, 1877, gave a true account of Calamity in its review of distinguished men and women, it did not take long for that lady to recover from her grief over Wild Bill. As reported by that paper she had "married and settled down in Custer City, South Dakota."[17] There may or may not have been any truth in that rumor, but at least someone was interested enough in her love life to venture such a statement.

The same year, from Nebraska came evidence of some husband or other and a child. Domestic drudgery must have held no charm for Calamity. She deserted not only her husband for a bull-whacker and her household duties for bull-whacking but she also deserted her offspring. An unsympathetic press said of her:

> She has now gone west with a bull-whacker to learn the trade. Her husband is not a violent mourner. She is a stubby customer, American and cussed. If she has any conscience she took it with her, and if she had any virtue her husband didn't know it. The child is now in good hands, and the painter is happy.[18]

A few years later from Montana came a tale of a husband and a new baby. The announcement read:

> Calamity Jane has settled down to domestic life on a ranch in Yellowstone Valley, below Miles City. She lives with her husband and has been blessed with a fine boy baby which she calls "little Calamity."[19]

When another paper carried similar news and added, "The Deadwood papers are eulogizing Calamity Jane and the recently born little Calamity,"[20] it seemed that

---

[17] *Cheyenne Daily Leader,* January 26, 1877.

[18] *Sidney* (Nebraska) *Telegraph,* August 4, 1877.

[19] *Semi-Weekly Miner* (Butte, Montana), December 6, 1882.

[20] *Yellowstone Journal* (Miles City, Montana), November 25, 1882.

at last some real evidence could be found about a child belonging to this notorious woman. A thorough search of the Deadwood papers for several months previous to the notice uncovered no mention of "little Calamity's" birth.[21]

There is ample evidence that during this period, Calamity Jane was mixed up in some manner with a young man named Robert Dorsett. In Livingston, Montana, as late as the middle of the twentieth century, she was remembered as living with him. Two old men, alive in 1951 and reputed to be honest citizens interested in history, plainly recalled Calamity and Dorsett. When one of them, Mr. George Simon,[22] was asked if Calamity were married when he knew her in Livingston, he replied that she was and to a Charlie Dorsett. He was mistaken about the first name, but mentioned the surname, Dorsett, without prompting. When plied further about the time, he said he had no special way of connecting their activities with any events which would give him a clue to the date. Upon further questioning about the legality of the marriage, he said that he knew nothing, except that the two lived together and he assumed they were married. A second Livingstonian, Mr. Fred Sumner,[23] younger than Mr. Simons, had more specific facts to give. Mr. Sumner remembered that in the early 1880's Robert Dorsett worked for him on his ranch in the Shields River valley and also on ranches on Boulder River. In 1886, Sumner was working for the Miles Company, where Calamity Jane bought supplies for her string of race horses.[24] One day he took her order for some feed to be delivered to the fairgrounds. Calamity rode with him, he recalled, and "talked as nice as any lady he ever saw—not rough at

---

[21] The *Yellowstone Journal* of December 12, 1882, three weeks after the notice had appeared about the birth of "Little Calamity," noted that Calamity was running a hurdy-gurdy house in Livingston.

[22] Interview with Mr. George Simon August, 1949.

[23] Interview with Mr. Fred Sumner August, 1949.

[24] It is doubtful if Calamity Jane ever owned any race horses. She may have claimed such or given that impression.

all." When they arrived at the fair-grounds Dorsett was there with her outfit and she introduced him to Mr. Sumner as her husband. Mr. Sumner surmised that, about 1880, Dorsett was fourteen, making him twenty when Calamity claimed him as her husband. She was then approximately thirty-four herself, fourteen years his senior. There is no reason to doubt the general truth of the story except perhaps the dates. A Livingston paper in September, 1887, mentioned "Calamity Jane, who a few years ago was a conspicuous figure in Livingston and other Yellowstone points."[25] It seems that if she had been in Livingston the year before, as Mr. Sumner indicated, the phrase "a few years ago" would not have been used by the paper. Although Calamity could possibly have been around in 1886 without the city editor's knowing it, the likelihood is not great. On the other hand, perhaps a year's breaking spell from her antics felt so good that it seemed several years since hearing and seeing her.

The Livingston city directory, published for the first time in 1904, listed a Robert H. Dorsett as having moved to Pueblo, Colorado. No occupation was given. A man from Bozeman in a story to a Butte paper in 1901 remarked that "Calamity Jane's name at this time is Mrs. Dorsett. She married a man of that name in Livingston some years ago and they parted soon afterwards."[26] The editor of the Livingston paper who wrote the obituary notice of Calamity said that "in the early 90's Calamity came to Livingston. She married a young man named Robert Dorsett with whom she lived a short time only."[27] In at least one edition, the *Autobiography* has the name Dorsett, photographed from longhand after the final signature. This indicates that someone else knew of her connection with him. It must have met her approval to have the name there, because she kept on selling the pamphlet. The diary which Jane Hickok

[25] *Livingston* (Montana) Enterprise, September 17, 1887.
[26] *Anaconda* (Butte, Montana) *Standard*, February 13, 1901.
[27] *Livingston* (Montana) *Post*, August 6, 1903.

McCormick presented as Calamity's contained the statement "I have been called the common law wife of King,
Conors, Wilson and Dorsett."[28] If the diary is *bona fide,*
then that is Calamity's admission of some relationship
with Dorsett. If the diary is forged it still shows that
the forger knew at least Calamity Jane was involved
with him.

It was while searching through the records of the
Park County Courthouse in Livingston for some sem-
blance of a Cannary-Dorsett marriage license that this
writer found another interesting document.[29] From its
contents it is obvious that the Dorsett incident soured
Calamity Jane neither on men nor on Livingston, for
in November, 1888, some arrest papers showed that she
and a man named Charles Townley, both unmarried,
were booked for fornication. They were judged not
guilty by a jury,[30] but that did not mean that they were
not living together.

Charles Townley was a familiar Livingston character
in the 1880's. In August, 1888, he was arrested for petty
larceny[31] and in January, 1889, he was found uncon-
scious from a dose of morphine. Pinned to him was a
note on which was written:

> I can't freeze to death. I have been ruined by
> a prostitute. She soaked my tools for whisky, and
> I could have made money by paper hanging and
> house painting. What little money I did get I bought
> whisky for the harlot. I curse the day we met, so
> I have poisoned myself.[32]

---

[28] Clarence Paine, p. 15.
[29] No record of any such marriage could be found, owing perhaps to the
fact that permanent records for most things did not begin until after
Montana Territory became Montana State in 1889. Calamity could
have legally married Dorsett in 1886 when Mr. Sumner knew them and
not have had the marriage recorded.
[30] Photostatic copies of the court record and the jury's verdict are reproduced on pages 87 and 88. The verdict was on a lined piece of tablet
paper, yellow with age.
[31] *Livingston Enterprise,* August 18, 1888.
[32] *Ibid.,* January 26, 1889.

A few days later he died and part of an account about him ran:

> To top the climax with his brain befuddled with the fumes of alcohol, he became infatuated with one of the lowest women of the town. He managed to eke out a miserable and drunken existence with the woman by doing some house painting.[33]

A pertinent question is, "Was the 'prostitute,' 'harlot' and 'one of the lowest women of the town' Calamity Jane?" She was definitely known to be a hard drinker, but whether she would have "soaked his tools" for liquor may be questioned. Her known promiscuity would have entitled her to any or all the above appellations, and her conduct with Townley three months previously would not exactly be a point for exoneration. A man of Townley's class might well have been associating with any number of disreputable women, and Calamity Jane could easily qualify as one of them. There is one mite of historical evidence which might help to identify Calamity as "the woman." Aikman enumerated her husbands and loves and his long impressive list included "a drunken painter in Livingston."[34] If Calamity Jane did marry or live with a painter in Livingston, it is not certain, but not unlikely, that the man was Townley.

Then there was Mr. Burk (with or without an *e*), the ubiquitous Mr. Clinton Burk. Various writers have placed him everywhere in Calamity's life, sometimes as her first husband, sometimes as her last, other times as her only legal husband, but always noted somewhere. He undoubtedly received the honor because of the place given him by Calamity in her *Autobiography*. He is the only man mentioned in that account as a husband. Here is her story of the romance that culminated in holy matrimony:

---

[33] *Ibid.*, February 2, 1889.
[34] Duncan Aikman, *Calamity Jane and the Lady Wildcats*, p. 109.

While in El Paso, (reached there in fall of 1884) I met Mr. Clinton Burk, a native of Texas, who I married in August 1885. As I thought I had travelled through life long enough alone and thought it was about time to take a partner for the rest of my days. We remained in Texas leading a quiet home life until 1889. On October 28th, 1887, I became the mother of a girl baby, the very image of its father, at least that is what he said, but who has the temper of its mother.

When we left Texas we went to Boulder, Colo., where we kept a hotel until 1893, after which we travelled through Wyoming, Montana, Idaho, Washington, Oregon, then back to Montana, then to Dakota, arriving in Deadwood, October 9th, 1895, after an absence of seventeen years.[35]

From the fall of 1884 until August, 1885, when Calamity said she was in El Paso and when anyone would assume her courtship with Mr. Burk was taking place, three short newspaper items from far-off Wyoming prove that she was a good seven hundred miles from her beloved in the Lone Star State. A Cheyenne paper under the column, "Local Mavericks," noted:

Calamity Jane, the noted female rustler of the Rocky Mountain region, who spent several months this summer in Buffalo (Wyoming), has again been heard from. She is leading a quiet life at Fort Washakie (Lander, Wyoming) this territory.[36]

A month later Calamity must have made a little excursion to Rawlins, because the paper said that "Calamity Jane, the noted and notorious, made famous by Ned Buntline, the border novelist, is in Rawlins,"[37] The

[35] *Autobiography*, p. 6.

[36] *Democratic Leader* (Cheyenne, Wyoming), November 25, 1884.

[37] *Carbon County Journal* (Rawlins, Wyoming), December 20, 1884.

whisky of that town may not have suited her, however, for in the spring of the following year she had "concluded to make Lander her permanent place of abode."[38]

That Calamity "remained in Texas leading a quiet home life until 1889" can readily be disputed. In October, 1885, two months after her alleged marriage to Burk, she was not in El Paso. According to an elaborate account in the newspaper "the hideous ruin" was settled in Lander.[39] Later she picked up a Mr. Steers as her paramour, and ran into court difficulties in Meeker, Colorado, when she charged him with beating her up.[40] Immediately after that the two appeared in Rawlins, where Calamity complicated her marital status by posing as Mrs. Martha King[41] while living with Mr. Steers but, according to her story ten years later, having actually been Mrs. Burk.

There are several vague references to a fellow named King. Calamity may have been involved with him, sufficiently at least so that she felt entitled to call herself Mrs. King. Frackelton mentioned that she had appeared in northern Wyoming in 1885, where she lived with a man named Frank King on a ranch on Powder River. The place was run as a horse ranch by the "76" outfit and King had charge of the horses.[42] Another account mentioned her husband as John King.[43] Furthermore, in the diary already mentioned, Calamity listed King as one of her common law husbands.[44]

Her post office name may have been Mrs. Martha King according to the *Carbon County Journal* of September 18, 1886, but the same paper seven weeks later

[38] *Democratic Leader,* March 21, 1885.
[39] *Cheyenne Daily Leader,* November 3, 1885. (Special correspondent from Lander, Wyoming, October 30, 1885.)
[40] *Carbon County Journal,* September 18, 1886, citing *Meeker* (Colorado) *Herald.*
[41] *Carbon County Journal,* September 18, 1886.
[42] Will Frackelton, *Sagebrush Dentist,* p. 125.
[43] *Casper* (Wyoming) *Tribune-Herald,* November 26, 1921.
[44] Clarence Paine, p. 15.

referred to her as Calamity Jane Steers.[45] It minced no words describing Steers. A few choice phrases it used about him were that he "deserves a hangmen's knot," "is a miserable stick," and "is one of the worthless curs unhung."[46]

Monogamous to the point of monotony, Calamity Jane was still Mrs. Steers one whole year later. Not only did she bear the same name, but she had been on a trip with Steers and was returning home with him to Rawlins. She told a reporter that she "was married to Mr. Steers in Rawlins two years ago and had lived there most of the time since."[47] With this in mind it is interesting to note that according to her *Autobiography,* five months later a girl baby, "the very image of its father, at least that is what he said," was born to Calamity and *Burk* in El Paso.

From 1890 to 1895, little or nothing is known of Calamity Jane. When she did reappear in 1895, it was in Deadwood, South Dakota, as Mrs. Burk. When and where she joined company with Burk is hard to say, but, as her former unions were of short duration, a likely supposition is that it had not been long before reaching Deadwood.

The two local newspapers gave glowing accounts of her "return home," but only scanty details of her husband. From the *Pioneer-Times* the following information is obtained:

> Mrs. Jane Burk . . . arrived in the City yesterday after an absence of sixteen years during which time she has been living quietly with her husband on a ranch in southeastern Montana. They drove across the country to Belle Fourche and Mrs. Burk came to Deadwood to do a little shopping and renew "auld acquaintances."[48]

---

[45] *Carbon County Journal,* November 6, 1886.
[46] *Ibid.,* September 18, October 30 and November 6, 1886.
[47] *Cheyenne Daily Leader,* June 21, 1887.
[48] *Pioneer-Times* (Deadwood, South Dakota), October 5, 1895.

The competing daily mentioned a little daughter with Calamity about nine years old. Calamity gave her own name as Mrs. M. Burk, the mother of two "bright little girls." She was reported to have been living the past summer with her husband on a ranch about fourteen miles from Ekalaka, Montana, but she did not like that kind of life.[49] Mr. Burk apparently joined his family for, three months later, when Calamity went on tour with the dime museum, one newspaper reported that Mr. Burk, having been offered a job, was going to accompany her to Minneapolis.[50] The departure notice a few days later made brief comment that "Calamity Jane and her husband, Mr. Burk, left yesterday for Minneapolis."[51]

McClintock gives a good account of Burk who, he said, came to Deadwood in company with Calamity and a bright little girl nine or ten years old. Burk found a job as a hack driver and proved himself competent. However, he soon became an embezzler by appearing to trust his customers and making excuses for not turning in his cash receipts. When he had accumulated one hundred and seventy dollars in that manner he absconded and was never heard of again.[52] A month after leaving Minneapolis with her husband Calamity visited Helena, Montana, selling her *Autobiography*. The newspaper referred to her as Mrs. Clement Burk, but did not mention her husband.[53] In the numerous newspaper

---

[49] *Black Hills* (Deadwood, South Dakota) *Daily Times,* October 5, 1895.

[50] *Ibid.,* January 9, 1896.

[51] *Ibid.,* January 16, 1896.

[52] John S. McClintock, p. 119. Mr. John Sohn said in an interview in August, 1949, that he had known Burk well. He always thought the man was a nice fellow and had disappeared because he was ashamed of being married to Calamity. The matter had never seemed important enough for him to investigate but he had drawn his own conclusions. When reminded of the story McClintock told, Mr. Sohn agreed that McClintock must be right, for he usually kept close tab on Deadwood pioneer characters and their associates.

[53] *Daily Independent* (Helena, Montana), September 18, 1896.

accounts that appeared subsequently over a period of years, indeed, Burk was never referred to as being in company with his wife.

The most provocative angle arising from the Burk-Cannary liaison is the one involving the daughter. If the child was about nine years old in October, 1895, as the Deadwood *Pioneer-Times* reported, the fact would fit well with Calamity's claim that she and Burk had a girl baby born October 28, 1887. But since that possibility has been shown to be remote, the best guess is that the child was Burk's daughter by another woman. Calamity insisted that the girl was her own, and stuck to that story even on her deathbed, when she talked of a daughter in North Dakota and hinted of an estrangement with her.[54]

Miss Estelline Bennett talked to Calamity and the little girl on the day of their arrival in Deadwood. Calamity told Miss Bennett that she wanted to put the child in a convent to get some schooling, but would have to have help from her Deadwood friends. The old-timers gave a benefit for her at the "Green Front," a disreputable hurdy-gurdy house. The affair was a great success and enough money poured in to take care of the child's entire education. When the "Green Front" turned the money over to Calamity, she treated the whole crowd to drinks for having been so kind. Forgetting all about the daughter, the mother got roaring drunk. The purse was rescued before it was too late, however, and the next day the child was taken away to St. Martin's Convent in Sturgis, a small town fifteen miles from Deadwood.[55]

The daughter remained at the convent only a short time. Details of her whereabouts were and are carefully guarded secrets. Quite possibly both she and Calamity realized that it was best for the outside world never to know of the relationship between them. The stigma of

[54] *Pioneer-Times,* August 2, 1903.
[55] Estelline Bennett, *Old Deadwood Days,* pp. 230-242.

Calamity even as a foster mother would be enough to prejudice society against the girl. Today she is a woman about sixty-five years old. Not long ago she wrote to the convent for the record of payments made to the school for her while she stayed there. This is one main channel which, if followed, might lead to solving questions about Calamity Jane which otherwise will remain mysteries. All of the sisters who taught at the school in 1895 and 1896 are now dead, but they did pass on information about the case which the present regime refuses to divulge.[56]

In addition to these men whose connection with Calamity Jane has been somewhat authenticated, there are rumors of many other men who had some part in her love life. The list is long. It goes back to 1862 when Lieutenant Washburne was mentioned.[57] Then in 1868, the prosperous Mr. White supposedly married Calamity in Denver.[58] A few others reported are Lieutenant Somers,[59] Sergeant Shaw[60] and Sergeant Siechrist[61] though information other than their names seems impossible to find. Whether any of these stories are true, it is impossible to say, but they do represent the public's idea of Calamity's interest in men.

---

[56] Interview with two nuns of St. Martin's Convent July 1949.
[57] *Cheyenne* (Wyoming) *Daily Sun,* July 7, 1877.
[58] Jessie Brown and A. M. Willard, *The Black Hills Trails,* p. 413.
[59] Aikman, p. 46.
[60] Harry "Sam" Young, *Hard Knocks,* p. 171.
[61] Stewart S. Holbrook, *Little Annie Oakley and Other Rugged People,* p. 32.

Chapter VII.

NURSING

Protestations of Calamity's devotion, good-will and ability as a nurse come from almost as loud a chorus of commentators as the acclamation she has received as an outstanding roisterer and swearer. A selection of the accounts of Calamity's services as a nurse is presented here to show the attitude of the community toward her services.

Brown and Willard give Calamity Jane credit for day and night selfless toil in the 1878 epidemic,[1] but the most colorful picture of the woman's work in that bad year appears in Estelline Bennett's *Old Deadwood Days:*

> And everyone of them was remembering those days in '78 when Calamity Jane alone took care of the smallpox patients in a crude log cabin pest house up in Spruce Gulch around behind White Rocks, the tall limestone peak over which the belated morning sun shines down on Deadwood Gulch. Smallpox was the most dreaded scourge of the frontier town. Usually people died because of dearth of nursing, of facilities for taking care of the sick, and bad sanitary conditions. For the same reasons, it spread with terrifying speed. Those who recovered came from their sick beds with marred faces. All that a town like Deadwood in '78 knew to do for smallpox patients was to set aside an isolated cabin and notify the doctor.
>
> There were half a dozen patients in the small log pest house in Spruce Gulch when Dr. Babcock made his first visit. He said they were all very sick and

---

[1] Jessie Brown and A. M. Willard, *The Black Hills Trails,* p. 415.

he was going back after supper. No one offered to go with him, but when he went back he found Calamity Jane there.

"What are you doing here?" he asked.

"Somebody's got to take care of 'em," she replied. "They can't even get 'emselves a drink of water when they want it. You tell me what to do, Doc, and I'll stay right here and do it."

"You'll probably get the smallpox," he warned her.

"Yes, I know. I'll have to take that chance. I can't leave them here to die all alone. Won't they have a better chance if I stay and do what you tell me?"

There was no question but what they would and he told her so. But he looked at her clear olive skin and the firm contours of her face and chin and reminded her that it was not only disease and death she risked. With women of Calamity Jane's sort beauty was as important almost as life itself. It was their stock in trade. Beauty and bravery were Calamity's best assets. It was doubtful if she would ever lose her courage but, without her beauty, what would she do with her life? He reminded her of this too. She took nothing into account except that half a dozen very sick men needed her services desperately, and she stayed. The charmed life that had persisted through Indian arrows, and guns, through desperate gun fights, various hazards and hardships, held her dark striking beauty for further destruction. She came unscathed through the long smallpox siege and most of her patients lived. Dr. Babcock believed that without her care not one of them could have pulled through.

WITH "SATAN"   Plate XV

Calamity Jane stands beside her horse "Satan" in this picture taken at the old mining settlement of Gilt Edge, Montana in about 1885. The photographer was the late Dr. W. A. Allen of Billings. Pioneer George Hays has said that this was Calamity Jane exactly as he remembered her. Historical Society of Montana photo.

She never left the pest cabin during those hard weeks except to make hurried trips down to Deadwood for supplies that the grocers gave her.[2]

Connelley, too, gives her general and specific credit for nursing activities, but dates the epidemic a year later:

She was a warm friend, ready to grubstake the pal who was "broke," to care for and nurse any down-and-out who needed it. She was equally quick to mother some homesick boy or punish the one who would torment him . . .

In 1879, fire swept Deadwood, and a little later, smallpox ravaged it. Calamity Jane laid aside her guns and became a nurse—an awkward one, but endlessly gentle and patient. Out of her own small resources, she took money for food and medicines for those too poor to buy their own. She worked long and bravely, going constantly from one house to another on her errands of kindness.[3]

Lewis Crawford insists that Calamity Jane received her nickname as a mark of affection from those to whom she ministered during the epidemic of 1878.

In 1878 a smallpox epidemic broke out in Deadwood, hundreds were bedfast from the scourge, and many died. It was here that this outcast woman, true to the better instincts of her sex, ministered day and night among the sick and dying, with no thought of reward or of what the consequences might be to herself. Her unselfish labors during this great calamity all but blotted out the past in the eyes of many, and the people gave her the name, "Calamity

---

[2] Estelline Bennett, *Old Deadwood Days,* p. 223.

[3] William Elsey Connelley, *Wild Bill and His Era,* pp. 188-189. See also O. W. Coursey, *Beautiful Black Hills,* p. 110.

Jane," as a mark of recognition if not affection; and by this name she has been since known throughout the West.[4]

D. Dee, whose memoirs, although discreetly incomplete, have a more objective tone than many others, similarly associates Calamity Jane's name with her nursing charity during the 1878 plague.

In the year 1878, eight men came down with smallpox, they were quarantined in a little shack on the shoulder of the mountain called "White Rocks." Calamity had volunteered to care for these men, of whom three died. She would yell down to the placer miners in the gulch below for anything she needed, and throw down a rope by which to send supplies. They would bring her what she required to the foot of the hill and she would haul them up hand over hand. Her only medicines were epsom salts and cream of tartar. When they died she wrapped them in a blanket and yelled to the boys to dig a hole. She carried the body to the hole and filled it up. She only knew one prayer, "Now I Lay Me Down to Sleep." This was the funeral oration she recited over the graves. But her good nursing brought five of these men out of shadow of death, and many more later on, before the disease died out.

Think of a trained nurse these days nursing eight men, working as cook, doctor, chambermaid, water boy, and undertaker, with the duties of a sexton throw in.

If anyone was sick in camp, it was, "send for Jane;" where Calamity was, there was Jane; and so she was christened Calamity Jane.[5]

---

[4] Lewis F. Crawford, *Rekindling Camp Fires*, p. 274.
[5] D. Dee, *Low Down on Calamity Jane*, p. 4.
    D. Dee, whose real name was Dora Dufran, owned a house of prostitution in Belle Fourche and Rapid City, South Dakota.

Holbrook, a skeptic of many Calamity legends, was completely convinced of the truth of these testimonials, and gives her full credit for her service to the sick.[6]

Sabin, too, remarks that Deadwood citizens later forgave Calamity her trespasses because of her concern to relieve suffering.

Some phases of Martha Jane Canary rechristened Calamity Jane are to be passed. But she it was who, while the smallpox ravaged Deadwood in 1878, like a Florence Nightingale of the battlefield week after week nursed from bed to bed and bunk to bunk throughout the gulch, took risks that no one else would take, and asked nothing in return. Deadwood never forgot this.

The woman in her was bound to come out in one way or another. She turned the same trick over at Pierre, where a settler family was practically abandoned in a quarantine for black diphtheria. Calamity broke the quarantine. From twenty dollars which she somehow accumulated she spent fifteen for food and medicine, crossed the deadline and stayed in the cabin until she was no longer needed there.[7]

Hoshier, Calamity's friend and pallbearer, whose account seems impartial, says: "She was a fine nurse. There wasn't anything she wouldn't do for anybody and whenever she had any money it went just the same way, easily and for the first fellow that asked for it."[8]

Stewart H. Holbrook, *Little Annie Oakley and Other Rugged People,* p. 34.

[7] Edwin Legrand Sabin, *Wild Men of the Wild West,* p. 339.
   Milner gives her full credit for unselfish service. He points out, however, apparently with some malice left over from his grandfather, California Joe, that Calamity thus entered cabins where she had never been welcome before. Joe E. Milner and Earle R. Forrest, *California Joe,* p. 231.

[8] *Great Falls* (Montana) *Leader,* July 16, 1906.

Calamity's funeral sermon included an account of her work in the 1878 epidemic, and an appreciation which places it in context as part of frontier life:

We are reminded today of the beginning of things in Deadwood and vicinity.

You walk today amid the improvements which have cost the labors of 25 years. You are fearless in all your enterprises today. In the other days you could not venture from your cabin without the rifle or revolver with which to defend yourself. You are surrounded by schools and churches and enjoy and appreciate these elements of a higher civilization.

The romance of the Black Hills has never been written. Some time there will come a writer who with the breadth of mind sufficient to comprehend the work you have done and the stirring events which have attended your labors, will write the romantic history of the Black Hills. When the romance is written whoever may be the heroes, Jane Burke will in all the deeds which kindness and charity dictated in those days be the heroine.

How often amid the snows of winter did this woman find her way to a lonely cabin of a miner who was suffering from the disease of those times and who felt sorely the need of food and medicine.

When the history of this country is written too much can not be said of the results of this woman's labors in helping you to build and to complete the work you had undertaken. As I think of her labors and voluntary sacrifices I hear the voice of Christ as he said: "Even as much as ye have done it unto the least of these my little ones, ye have done it unto me."[9]

---

[9] *Pioneer-Times* (Deadwood, South Dakota), August 5, 1903.

These accounts are unanimous in crediting her contemporaries' conviction that Calamity could be called upon for aid whenever anyone was sick and in need of help. If she were sober, she would go immediately to them and take care of their needs. If she were drunk, she would sober up and be ready to care for the sick the next day.

Aikman quotes what he refers to as a "leading Black Hills anti-traditionalist," which may be translated as a professional debunker, to the effect that Calamity's nursing amounted to no more than taking "the boys" a few drops of liquor when she had too much. Aikman also insists that upon visiting her territory and talking with dozens of her contemporaries he found only one who had positive knowledge of anyone whom Calamity had nursed.[10] This writer, however, twenty-five years later on visiting the same area, was able to find several people who remembered well and definitely the specific details of some of Calamity's nursing exploits.

Mr. Charles Fales of Fort Pierre, an old pioneer still living, related the following story about Calamity Jane's nursing his sister while the latter was ill with mountain fever. Miss Fales was one of the very few "ladies" in Fort Pierre and the men in town had great respect for her. When they heard that she was ill they went to Calamity Jane who was in town at the time getting ready to take a bull-train to Rapid City. They asked her if she would change into a dress and go to nurse Miss Fales and take good care of her. They also coached her on how to behave at the Fales' residence: there must be no drinking, no smoking, and no rough language. Calamity Jane agreed to act circumspectly, cleaned up nicely and tripped up to Miss Fales' house. For three weeks she nursed Miss Fales capably and untiringly until her charge was well again. Then Calamity asked her, "Do you still need me or are you well enough to take care of yourself?" Miss Fales said that she

---

[10] Duncan Aikman, *Calamity Jane and the Lady Wildcats*, p. 108.

would be able to manage very well by herself and thanked her profusely for the wonderful service she had rendered. Mr. Fales recalled that as soon as the thanks had been extended Calamity Jane streaked out of the house and apparently to the nearest bar; when he had occasion to go up town shortly after that he saw her on the street so drunk that "if she had tipped her head forward even the slightest bit she would have fallen." It seemed very much as if she were desperately trying to catch up on the drinking she had missed while caring for Miss Fales, for Mr. Fales remarked that during the last few days at his home Calamity Jane seemed very nervous and "jumpy."[11] Calamity may have been the "angel of mercy" in many instances but there was a limit to the amount of time during which she could abstain from liquor. One of her friends set the limit at six weeks,[12] which might well have been giving her the benefit of any doubt.

Then there is the pioneer Robinson family of Deadwood whose experience with Calamity Jane as a nurse has been noted many times by both historians and sensational writers.[13] In the late 1870's the six children of the Harry Robinson family were stricken with "black diphtheria." Without being invited, but because she was extremely fond of the sick children and particularly of one little girl, Calamity Jane walked into the home and took charge of all the young patients. Three of the children including the little girl died. Of the surviving three children, one was Charles Robinson who years later had the dubious honor of burying his former benefactress at Mt. Moriah Cemetery in Deadwood.[14]

George Simon, a very feeble but mentally alert old man who in 1949 still owned and operated a ready-to-wear shop in Livingston, Montana, remembered much

---

[11] Interview with Mr. Charles Fales August 1949.

[12] D. Dee, p. 7.

[13] Duncan Aikman, p. 70; John S. McClintock, *Pioneer Days in the Black Hills*, p. 118; Jessie Brown and A. M. Willard, p. 415.

[14] Interview with Mrs. Mary Robinson August 1949.

about Calamity Jane—what a good woman she was and how she saved his life when he was sick. A speech impediment frustrated him to the point where he started crying with emotion and kept repeating what a wonderful woman she was and what a good friend she was when he needed her help and how she saved his life.[15]

With few exceptions, writers who usually give no credence to most Calamity tales are more than willing to credit her with at least rough abilities as a nurse. However, one question should be asked: "Why did the *Black Hills Daily Times* not 'sing her praises' during the times when the smallpox epidemics struck Deadwood?" Dozens of writers mention her good deeds at this time. In the late 1870's there were several sieges of the dreaded disease which swept through the town with varying degrees of severity. Yet, in the available files of the *Times* which begin July 1877 and continue for several years without a single missing issue, there is no reference directly or indirectly to the "Black Hills Florence Nightingale" in the role of nurse. It might be that the editor of the *Times* was prejudiced against Calamity and refused to give her the public recognition she deserved. This editor was definitely "anti-Calamity" for in September, 1877, items in two different editions scoffed at the editor of the rival *Pioneer* for allowing her to appear as a heroine. His contempt for such publicity given her is shown by a sarcastic notice:

> The reason that we failed to "discover the peculiarities" of the *Pioneer's* "heroine of the Hills" [Calamity] is easily explained. We refuse to cultivate the same intimacy with her that the presiding genius of that romantic sheet did.[16]

Even if the *Times* editor did not like Calamity, it is unlikely that the reading public would have allowed him to ignore her if she had rendered the services and

---

[15] Interview with Mr. George Simon August 1949.
[16] *Black Hills Daily Times* (Deadwood, South Dakota), September 22, 1877.

performed the sacrifices related by so many writers. Unfortunately, the files for the *Pioneer* are missing for this period. But the editor obviously did romantically refer to Calamity or he would not have provoked such reactions from the editor of the *Times*. For the year prior to the 1878 epidemic there is one single edition of the *Pioneer* still extant. It contains an article which shows that Calamity gained a reputation as a nurse soon after she first arrived in Deadwood. The heading of the account was "Calamity Jane as Nurse" and reads:

> The man Warren, who was stabbed on lower Main St. Wednesday night, is doing quite well under the care of Calamity Jane, who has kindly undertaken the job of nursing him. There's lots of humanity in Calamity, and she is deserving of much praise for the part she has taken in this particular case.[17]

All these bits of information about Calamity as a nurse may fit together to give a more reasonable view of the part she played in that profession. For the many stories handed down second- and third-hand there must have originally been some basis in fact, or they would not be so numerous and so positive. In addition to these tales, personal interviews with reliable people show that there were a few people, at least, whom she did care for: Miss Fales, a lone woman in a rough frontier community; the six little Robinson children; and a friend of hers, Mr. George Simon. Finally there is the news item in the *Pioneer* referring to her taking an interest in the case of a man "stabbed on lower Main St." Those three "sources" the newspaper, the personal interviews and the handed down tales which all writers give indicate that she did nurse and care for some sick people. But with the omission of her name in the *Times* in connection with the smallpox epidemics, the logical conclusion

[17] *Pioneer-Times*, June 20, 1951, citing the *Pioneer* (Deadwood, South Dakota), July 13, 1876.

takes a different turn. It may then be assumed that off and on throughout her life Calamity nursed sick people, particularly her friends and unfortunates, but never a whole community nor to the extent of becoming a heroine. Even Calamity made no boast in her *Autobiography* of her services during the epidemic. She left that to the fantastic imagination of the frontiersman.

AT LEWISTOWN   Plate XVI

Years of wandering and dissipation were taking their toll on Calamity Jane when this picture was taken on the main street of Lewistown in about 1899. She was standing by a wagon-load of wool when the late Mrs. E. G. Worden took the picture. Reproduced through courtesy of J. Leonard Jennewein, Mitchell, S. Dak.

Chapter VIII.

BULL-WHACKER

According to the accounts of most commentators, Calamity Jane was an expert bull-whacker. A few writers, however, lump this story of her bull-whacking accomplishments with the general hoax of her being a scout and a guide. One of the doubting narrators is Aikman. He refuses to credit her with more than a sort of playful taking-over of a bull-team on simple and easy tasks, such as relieving a tired whacker.[1] However, it was found that the few old-timers left around Rapid City, Pierre and Fort Pierre, South Dakota, honestly believed that she had been an outstanding driver.

Calamity's *Autobiography* states:

> In 1879 I went to Fort Pierre and drove trains from Rapid City to Fort Pierre for Frank Witcher, then drove teams from Fort Pierre to Sturgis for Fred Evans. This teaming was done with oxen as they were better fitted for the work than horses, owing to the rough nature of the country.[2]

There may be some truth in that paragraph. Calamity was in and around Fort Pierre during 1879 and 1880. Several short newspaper items prove that she was no stranger there. The *Yankton Press* noted that she had left that city on the steamer, Dakotah, for Fort Pierre[3] and, a year later, the Fort Pierre local commented that she had just come in from the Black Hills.[4] It is not impossible that, between her wanderings here and there in the Dakotas and Wyoming, she took three or four

---

[1] Duncan Aikman, *Calamity Jane and the Lady Wildcats*, p. 53.

[2] *Autobiography*, p. 5.

[3] *Black Hills Daily Pioneer* (Deadwood, South Dakota), May 29, 1879, citing the *Yankton* (South Dakota) *Press*.

[4] *Weekly Signal* (Fort Pierre, South Dakota), July 21, 1880.

weeks off occasionally to make a trip with a bull-team. No one claims she was a steady worker but there must have been times when she needed money and "whacking" was one way of earning it.

Her reference to Fred Evans is entirely in line with facts. As early as June, 1877, and for several years after, the papers ran ads for his freight line which was in the area where Calamity Jane claimed she worked for him. One account said: "Fred Evans, senior member of the Fort Pierre and Black Hills Transportation Company, left for points along the route between here and Fort Pierre, to expedite the travel of the many mule and ox teams of his line on the way between the Missouri River and Deadwood."[5] In addition to her being in the right place at the right time working for the right man, her familiarity with the fact that oxen "were better fitted for the work than horses, owing to the rough nature of the land" substantiates her story a little more. The objection may be raised that anyone would know that fact, and yet, there were equally obvious things in her fictitious scouting stories that she did not know.

Since bull-whacking was one profession to which Calamity probably belonged, a description of the work and the other details of it may help to put her in a setting where she had a recognized place. Mr. Charles Fales,[6] who is considered an authority on the subject of bullwhacking, recalled seeing her as a whacker off and on over a period of time from the year 1881, when he first arrived in Pierre, until 1889 when the railroad was extended to Rapid City. Although Mr. Fales was not a bull-whacker, he was familiar with the history and the duties of the occupation and was able to give the following information.

A bull-whacker was simply a person who "whacked" the bulls with a long whip to make them go. The covered wagons which carried goods were drawn by horses

---

[5] *Daily Champion* (Deadwood, South Dakota), June 2, 1877.
[6] Interview with Mr. Charles Fales August 1949.

BULL TRAIN

Plate XVII

This picture of a bull train on the main street of Miles City was taken in 1880 by the late L. A. Huffman, early day photographer. It is reproduced through the courtesy of his daughter, Mrs. Ruth Huffman Scott. Research reveals that Calamity Jane was in Miles City in 1883, and her skill as a bull-whacker is not doubted by historians.

or oxen. Oxen were the preferred beasts, as Calamity explained, but the phrase "bull-whacking" always persisted. They were slow beasts and needed constant prodding, but they were not so incorrigible as other animals and they were void of original ideas. They were steady, tireless plodders that ate up the miles with a slow never-changing gait.

The Chicago and Northwestern Railroad, pushing west from Chicago, reached Pierre, South Dakota in 1879, and connected that town with the East. As a terminal point for the railroad, Pierre became an important freight center for goods brought into and out of Rapid City and the rich mining fields of the Black Hills. The trail from Pierre to Rapid City covered a distance of one hundred fifty miles, and on the average twenty-one days were consumed in covering the distance. Ten teams of oxen were hitched together and pulled three covered wagons. Such a group was known as a bull-train and was kept in order by the whackers. In 1878, a chronicler reported that Calamity Jane had offered to bet she could "knock a fly off an ox's ear with a sixteen-foot whip-lash three times out of five."[7] By the time she was freighting out of Pierre in 1879 and the 1880's her effectiveness probably had risen to five times out of five. Ordinarily, ten trains traveled together, making a total of two hundred oxen, thirty wagons, ten whackers plus the wagon boss, night herder and cook. The first wagon was called the lead wagon, the second the swing, and the third the trail. One thousand pounds of freight were allowed per oxen head and the weight was distributed in the wagons, thirteen thousand pounds, four thousand and three thousand, respectively. The ideal load was that of "shoes" for the Homestake Mining Company. "Shoes" were large heavy pieces of iron which fit on the bottom of the crushers and were used for smashing the ore. These

Horatio N. Maguire, *The Coming Empire*, p. 65.

weighty objects were packed in the bottom of the wagons, allowing much space on top for lighter, more bulky goods. Such an arrangement gave the desired poundage without cumbersome piling up over the body of the wagon. When the caravan carried feed for the oxen, the number of days on the road was shortened because only abbreviated grazing periods were required. But most wagon bosses preferred to use all the space for freight, even though it meant taking longer camping time. Regard for the ability and health of the animals, in addition to personal comfort of the crew, made it necessary to set up a strict schedule for work, rest and meals. To follow this routine meant that the crew must rise early in the morning for the four-hour march from four to eight. An eight-hour rest and grazing period ensued from eight in the morning until four in the afternoon when the sun was hottest. The train moved on again to complete the second half of the eight hour day from four in the afternoon until eight in the evening. During the night, the night herder was in charge of the camp. Those evenings were times for frolic and good fellowship. The whackers gathered around the fire to sing and "out tall-talk" each other. There was time for a drink or two, though care had to be taken lest over-indulgence incapacitate the party and bring trouble to the whole caravan. Real revelry was left until the end of the line. And what did the bull-whackeress earn for her labors? A dollar a day and board when she ate with the outfit.

The region through which the route passed was called the Great American Desert, large sections of which were gumbo flats. Those stretches made for good traveling in dry weather but when the rains came those same flats turned into seas of a slimy, sticky substance that stuck to the wheels of the wagons and added tons of weight to the already heavy load. The hoofs of the oxen became so loaded that the animals were exhausted and finally bogged down completely. Such times were

CALAMITY AND FRIENDS   Plate XVIII

Calamity Jane's interest in men was apparently boundless. This animated
picture was taken in Denver, and she is shown with C. S. (Mountain
Charlie) Stobie and Captain Jack Crawford, one-time chief of the U. S. Army
Scouts. There has been some question as to whether or not this is the real
Calamity Jane. (See Picture Note No. 1 in the back of the book). Denver
Public Library photo.

extremely hard also on the bull-whackers,[8] and the fact that Calamity Jane made those trips not once but at least several times shows that she was a hardy character.

This method of earning a living, to which Calamity occasionally resorted, she began early in life. According to McClintock, who was in Deadwood at the time, she made more than one trip to Cheyenne as a bull-whacker in 1876. Commenting on her skill with the whip, he said: "Although I never happened to witness any of her cruel performances with a twenty-foot bull whip, it was generally conceded that she was an expert with that instrument of animal torture."[9] It appears that she could work as well as crack the whip, for after her Deadwood-Cheyenne run she was promoted to assistant wagon boss.[10]

In the 1880's others saw her engaged in this same occupation. Mrs. M. J. Schubert, who came to Pierre from Wisconsin in 1883, remembered that several times she saw Calamity walking down the street beside the teams with her whip in hand.[11] John Boland, who knew her, saw her in 1883 or 1884 at Viewfield in Elm Creek Valley, sixty miles east of Deadwood. She had thirty ox teams, of ten oxen each, freighting between Fort Pierre and the Black Hills.[12] Mrs. G. P. Dow saw Calamity Jane in the spring of 1889 at a store in Tubtown, Wyoming, driving an ox team. Wearing a brown skirt, a buckskin hunting jacket, a man's felt hat and

---

[8] The above four paragraphs with exception of two sentences, one cited in footnote seven, were dictated by Mr. Fales. He often is consulted by the South Dakota Historical Society on matters of local history because of his good memory and reliable stories. Several years ago he narrated the same material to a historian who confused things when his article was published. Mr. Fales was eager that this information should be recorded somewhere accurately because very little has been written on the subject. It is the desire of this author to give the facts as Mr. Fales gave them to her. Much editing had to be done but the details are exactly as given by the old man.

[9] John S. McClintock, *Pioneer Days in the Black Hills*, p. 117.

[10] *Sidney* (Nebraska) *Telegraph*, August 7, 1877.

[11] Interview with Mrs. M. J. Schubert August 1949.

[12] Nolie Mumey, *Calamity Jane*, p. 54.

heavy laced shoes, Calamity took her seat on the wagon, cracked her long bull-whip over the backs of the leaders and drove off. As a bull-whacker she could lash out with her voice as well as her whip.[13]

How a person of Calamity Jane's temperament could become proficient at a job as slow moving, tedious, boring and tiring as bull-whacking must have been has never been explained. The train advanced at the most seven miles a day over the endless prairies where the distance to the horizon was twice as far as a day's travel. After those trips, there is good reason to believe that the explosions and reverberations that followed were twice as great as they would have been normally. But as with "scouting" her interest in bull-whacking apparently was closely connected with her interest in men.

[13] "John Edmund Boland, River Man," *South Dakota State Historical Collections,* 1947, Vol. XXIII, p. 216.

Chapter IX.

SHOW GIRL

It would not be correct to call Calamity Jane an actress, and yet, she made two different stage appearances at large cities in both the Middle West and the East. The first series of performances took place during the winter of 1896, the second five years later in the summer of 1901. The concluding two paragraphs of Calamity's *Autobiography* mention briefly how she started on the stage.

My arrival in Deadwood after an absence so many years created quite an excitement among my many friends of the past, to such an extent that a vast number of the citizens who had come to Deadwood during my absence who had heard so much of Calamity Jane and her many adventures in former years were anxious to see me. Among the many whom I met were several gentlemen from eastern cities, who advised me to allow myself to be placed before the public in such a manner as to give people of the eastern cities an opportunity of seeing the Woman Scout who was made so famous through her daring career in the West and Black Hill countries.

An agent of Kohl & Middleton, the celebrated Museum men came to Deadwood, through the solicitation of the gentleman whom I had met there and arrangements were made to place me before the public in this manner. My first engagement began at the Palace Museum, Minneapolis January 20th, 1896, under Kohl & Middleton's management.[1]

---

[1] Autobiography, p. 7.

Mr. Middleton of Kohl and Middleton's Palace Museum went to Deadwood in person to persuade Calamity to tour through various cities exhibiting herself to the curious public. Quite probably, as she said, she attracted his attention after the enthusiastic reception she received upon her return to Deadwood the previous October. Her garb for the act in which she appeared was a handsome male attire of buckskin trousers and jacket. In addition, she was rigged out with all imaginable accompanying wild west accouterments. John Sohn, a local Deadwood shoemaker, had the job of shoeing the aspirant museum heroine. When Middleton visited the shop to see about ordering some appropriate boots, Sohn proudly exhibited several pairs which he thought were excellent samples. Middleton explained that he wanted boots with very high heels. Sohn showed the highest ones he had but still they were not high enough. When he remarked that Calamity could not walk if he made the heels any higher, Middleton assured him that it did not matter since all she had to do was stand. Her performance required no walking. The shoemaker made the boots for eleven dollars but was not surprised when Calamity did not pay for them. Many months later one of her friends who owned a local jewelry store settled the bill. He hated to see Sohn stuck for the boots, and as a long-time friend of Calamity Jane he wanted to put her credit in good standing.[2]

When word of this venture of Martha Cannary broke in Deadwood some considered it a joke but all made comments. The papers bustled with news. One account told that her itinerary included Minneapolis, Chicago, Philadelphia, New York and other cities, her appearances not exceeding two weeks in each. Mentioning that she did some splendid shooting when she practiced with a Winchester rifle, the newspaper went on to brag that although it was fifteen years since she had handled a gun, at one hundred paces she put five bullets out of

---

[2] Interview with Mr. John Sohn July 1949.

eight shots in a six-inch bull's eye.[3] A week later another item told of a contract for eight weeks with a fifty-dollar-per-week salary and all expenses. Calamity and her husband, Mr. Burk, left Deadwood January 15 to open her engagement at the Palace Museum in Minneapolis five days later.[4]

That Calamity Jane spent some time in show business is amply proven by a small advertisement on the theater page of the *Minneapolis Journal.* Alongside a tiny sketch of a ferocious looking woman appeared these words:

KOHL & MIDDLETON
PALACE MUSEUM
WEEK BEGINNING MON. JAN. 20

The famous woman scout of the Wild West. Heroine of a thousand thrilling adventures. The Terror of evildoers in the Black Hills! The comrade of Buffalo Bill and Wild Bill Hickok. See this famous woman and hear her graphic descriptions of her daring exploits.

A Host of Other Attractions

A Big Stage Show

That's All—One Dime—That's All[5]

Just how long Calamity Jane stayed at the Palace is hard to determine. The following week the museum advertisement in the newspaper ballyhooed another woman, Madamoiselle Peanka who did amazing feats in the cage with fierce man-eating African lions.[6] Whether Calamity remained as one of the performers included in the "Host of Other Attractions" is anyone's guess.

---

[3] *Black Hills Daily Times* (Deadwood, South Dakota), January 9, 1896.
[4] *Ibid.,* January 16, 1896.
[5] *Minneapolis* (Minnesota) *Journal,* January 20, 1896.
[6] *Ibid.,* January 27, 1896.

If it be assumed that Calamity continued on her circuit, the next logical jump was to Chicago, geographically the closest large city. One newspaper article in Deadwood earlier made the statement that Calamity would open in Minneapolis December 13 and in Chicago January 15.[7] Although those dates were changed, it shows that she originally expected to stay in Minneapolis two weeks and then go on to the next stand. With that in mind, a thorough search was made through the files of the *Chicago Tribune* for any mention of Calamity Jane's appearing in a dime museum there or of some gossip concerning her. Nothing was found. This lack of evidence might mean that Calamity Jane by-passed Chicago on her way to points east, although that is unlikely, or that she lost her major billing and continued without any publicity. But those familiar with her personality would probably agree that her name could not be found because the Minneapolis engagement was the last of her dime museum career. The chances are that she was not able to stay away from her liquor and conform to the restrictions imposed upon her by the management. One writer of Calamity stories wrote that she invaded not only Chicago but St. Louis, Kansas City and many other stations. Where he obtained his knowledge he did not reveal.[8]

The first authentic news that she was back in her old haunts appeared in a Deadwood paper of June 6, 1896. The notice mentioned that she had returned from the East and planned to reside permanently in Newcastle, Wyoming. It stated that youths who had devoured nonsensical yarns about her exploits had found an opportunity to "feast their eyes" upon her. The article went on to say that the public had gazed at her, simply an ordinary woman, and had lost its interest in her. It ended with the statement that she had filled all of her engagements in the eastern cities.[9] Despite the

[7] *Black Hills Daily Times,* December 12, 1895.
[8] Aikman, *Calamity Jane and the Lady Wildcats,* p. 119.
[9] *Pioneer-Times* (Deadwood, South Dakota), June 6, 1896.

Copyrighted, 1885, by BEADLE AND ADAMS. Entered at the Post Office at New York, N. Y., as Second Class Mail Matter. Feb. 11, 1885.

Vol. V. $2.50 a Year.   Published Weekly by Beadle and Adams,   Price, Five Cents.   No. 57.
No. 98 WILLIAM ST., NEW YORK.

DEADWOOD DICK ON DECK;

Or, CALAMITY JANE, The Heroine of Whoop-Up.

By E. L. Wheeler.

CHARACTER IN FICTION   Plate XIX

This pulp cover is typical of the fiction which Calamity Jane inspired during her lifetime. This five-cent weekly publication was produced in New York, and this one is dated Feb. 11, 1885. When Calamity Jane became a "show girl" several years later, she became even more a romantic figure to eastern writers. This has continued through the years, and even Hollywood has added its touch. Reproduced through courtesy of J. Leonard Jennewein, Mitchell, S. Dak.

last statement, absence of any other proof indicates that it was probably untrue. There are not even hand-me-down stories from voluble old pioneers mentioning that they or anyone else saw Calamity Jane in the dime museums of the East. Had she "filled all of her engagements," certainly a vestige of a story would remain today. If she did not follow the suggested schedule of appearances, then the time from her Minneapolis engagement to her arrival in Newcastle, Wyoming, a period of five months, may be accounted for in some other way. With her aimless attitude toward life, Calamity was probably in no hurry to go anywhere in particular, and she may have spent several months roaming through the Middle West enroute "home." The next five years of her life are a blank in the records, but she apparently remained in the West, settling at the little mining camp of Horr, Montana, near Livingston.

Calamity Jane's next venture as a show attraction was in 1901. In that year the Pan-American Exposition at Buffalo, New York, was in full swing. The promoters for the midway planned to add to their attractions a wild-west woman straight from the cow country. They sent Mrs. Josephine Brake, novelist and newspaper writer, to Montana to inveigle Calamity into going East to assume the role. The editor of the *Livingston Post* accompanied the journalist to Horr, where they found Calamity lying on a dirty bunk in a negro house of ill repute, sick and half-dead from a long drunk. If Mrs. Brake had known what she was letting herself in for she would have turned around and traveled home alone, a happy woman. Instead, she talked Calamity Jane into going to Buffalo, evading the real issue and promising her plenty of money, a palatial home and good company.[10] Mrs. Brake and her charge rode the Northern Pacific on the trip between Livingston and St. Paul. Calamity, who knew how to take advantage of a situation and always liked to play the part of an untamed

---

[10] *Livingston* (Montana) *Post,* August 6, 1903.

frontier woman, had a wonderful time. She promised
Mrs. Brake that she would not take a drink without
first telling her chaperon, and she kept her word. Every
time she took a drink she told Mrs. Brake. The only
trouble was that the telling became more frequent as
the journey progressed. When the two arrived in St.
Paul, Calamity was still going strong, but Mrs. Brake
showed signs of considerable strain. Reporters met them
at the hotel and had a field day interviewing the strange
pair.[11]

In what capacity Calamity Jane thrilled, frightened
or shocked her audiences on the midway at the Buffalo
Exposition is known either from accounts written years
after the exposition or from hearsay. An old-timer, Mr.
W. H. Newcom of Miles City, saw her performance and
described it thirty-three years later in the *Miles City
Daily Star*. He told vivid details about the barker who
introduced her act. This master of ceremonies, speaking
through a large megaphone, captivated the audience
with tales about the famous character who was going
to perform. After a great fan-fare and bugle calls,
Calamity "came 'tearing into the ring' on horseback,
buckskins, boots and guns, 'and stole the show'." Mr.
Newcom attended this exhibition with some pious eastern relatives. Learning that the cowgirl was a former
Montana acquaintance of his, they insisted upon meeting her. Worried and trembling at what this western
character might do and say to startle his sedate relatives, Newcom led them back stage for an introduction. All ended well for Calamity put on a most ladylike act.[12]

A different story is told by Wilstach. According to
him, Calamity began her eastern career in a small house
built on the electric route to Niagara Falls. Here she
sold her *Autobiography* and to advertise her scheme she
drove an eight-horse team through the streets of Buf-

[11] *St. Paul* (Minnesota) *Dispatch)*, July 13, 1901.
[12] *Miles City* (Montana) *Daily Star*, May 24, 1934.

BUFFALO BILL CODY   Plate **XX**

This colorful western showman has said he loaned Calamity Jane money "for old time's sake" to get home after her disastrously sodden Pan-American Exposition trip to Buffalo in 1901. It appears she got at least as far as Chicago on his money. Buffalo Bill, like most oldtimers, was tolerant of Calamity Jane's behavior, and regarded her as a symbol of the rugged Old West. Historical Society of Montana photo.

falo. For some reason the plan did not turn out well, so she appeared in an act on the midway of the exposition.[13]

An article about her death in the *Livingston Post* on August 6, 1903, had a brief note concerning her work at the exposition. It read that "at Buffalo, Calamity was given a job driving a six horse team to a coach in the midway."

The reason why Calamity "resigned" from her position to head west again is unknown. It might have been trouble over the royalty from the sale of her *Autobiography;* more likely it was too much drinking and squabbles with the authorities. One account recalled that after imbibing a little too much she "knocked out a Buffalo policeman. She was arrested but was shortly released."[14] An even more picturesque version reported that "drunk and fighting to the last gasp with the exposition officer Calamity was shooting the midway up."[15] Buffalo Bill was quoted by a Bozeman newspaper as having said: "I expect she was no more tired of Buffalo than the Buffalo police were of her, for her sorrows seemed to need a good deal of drowning." He went on to say that "she wanted money to get West again. Well, of course, she was one of the pioneers. For old time's sake, you know—."[16] The implication was that he bought her a ticket or at least gave some financial help. Being the great showman that he was, Buffalo Bill would no doubt make a bid for this kind of publicity, whether or not it was true. At least he let it be believed that he had furnished her with a ticket and expense money for her return to Montana. Reportedly she made things lively at several stops along the way.[17]

[13] Frank J. Wilstach, *Wild Bill Hickok*, p. 258.
[14] Livingston Post, August 6, 1903.
[15] Duncan Aikman, *Calamity Jane and the Lady Wildcats*, p. 122.
[16] *Avant Courier* (Bozeman, Montana), August 7, 1903.
[17] *Montana Weekly Record* (Helena), June 3, 1902.

There is no way of telling just when she left the Exposition City. A newspaper of October 2 noticed her in Chicago, so her departure from Buffalo probably was sometime in September. This item reported that several Montanans saw Calamity on the midway at the exposition. She had a chance meeting in Chicago with an old acquaintance from whom she begged carfare back to Montana. She had placed herself on exhibition in Chicago trying but failing to earn enough for train fare, hoped that the friend would pity her. However, if he refused her she was prepared to return "hobo fashion."[18] To give Buffalo Bill benefit of the doubt concerning his charitable gift to a "lady in distress," it may be said that her financial distress in Chicago does not mean that he had not given her more than ample funds for the whole trip. She could well have spent the entire amount while in Chicago and then started either working or begging.

An April, 1902, Livingston paper noted that she was in town again, giving the impression of being tired of the eastern cities and of the people who lived there. That town must have looked good to her. The people were the same, the bars were the same and the jails were the same. The Buffalo Exposition was over and Calamity Jane was home to stay.[19]

---

[18] *Fergus County Argus* (Lewistown, Montana), October 2, 1901.
[19] *Livingston Post,* April 24, 1902.

Chapter X.

JAIL

It can be said without reservation that Calamity Jane knew more about jails and related subjects than nursing, scouting, trouping or maybe even bull-whacking or any of the other careers attributed to her by her many chroniclers. To give variety to the discussion, such topics as bail, arrest, warrant, trial or any brush with the authorities will be considered along with jail.

The first contemporary evidence in print that Calamity Jane came to grips with the law was in 1876 at the youthful age of twenty-four. No mention was made of the reason for her detainment in the Cheyenne jail but she was reported to be rejoicing over her "release from durance vile." So happy was she with her freedom that she "borrowed" a horse and buggy and drove ninety miles to a neighboring army fort. When the gentleman who was sent after the conveyance arrived, she begged him not to arrest her and, as he had no authority to do so, he merely took charge of the outfit.[1] A year later when Calamity tried to borrow a rig at another shop in the same town the owner refused, recalling the previous ordeal. A notice in the paper commented at the time that after her joy ride a year earlier she had been booked for larceny but the prosecution had not pressed the case.[2]

Under the heading of "Cullings from Territorial News" an amusing short notice appeared in a Miles City newspaper in 1883 that "Kibble and Calamity Jane, charged with selling liquor to the Indians, got free owing to a technical error in the complaint."[3] The incident

---

[1] *Cheyenne* (Wyoming) *Daily Leader,* June 20, 1876.
[2] *Ibid.,* July 7, 1877.
[3] *Yellowstone Journal* (Miles City, Montana), March 3, 1883.

83

could have happened anywhere in Montana, for the Territory had numerous Indian reservations. Selling liquor to the Indians was an easy way to make unlawful profit.

Two years later a Rawlins paper gave a spirited account of Calamity in action:

> Calamity Jane became endowed with the ambition to meet any and all comers in the fistic arena last Saturday and accordingly loaded up with a more than average supply of "Elbow crooker" and started out. The first one to share honors with her was one Blanche Daville whom Calamity sent to grass on the first round. The next comer, however, proved too much for her, it being none other than one of the guardians of the peace who placed the gentle Maggie in durance vile until Monday morning when Edgerton scooped in the stakes and gate receipts amounting to nineteen dollars and ninety-five cents.[4]

What seems to be a paraphrase of this episode appeared in the Miles City paper two weeks later. "Calamity Jane has been heard from again. This time she bobbed up serenely at Rawlins, got drunk and knocked a frail sister out of time for which she was arrested and fined ten dollars and costs."[5]

In September, 1886, at Meeker, Colorado, Calamity Jane swore out a warrant for a fellow named Steers, a man acting in the capacity of her husband. At the trial she charged that he had stabbed her with the handle of a butcher knife and hit her on the lip with a rock. After being fined, he "hit the trail" but had not gone far before he realized that he needed Calamity

[4] *Carbon County Journal* (Rawlins, Wyoming), July 25, 1885.

[5] *Yellowstone Journal,* August 8, 1885.

to cheer him on his journey and so went back after her. They both started out afoot, Jane carrying the pack.[6]

The congenial pair probably hiked north, for the next month the Rawlins paper mentioned that Calamity Jane was in the local "bastille." She and Steers got into a drunken quarrel. The lady went in search of an officer but was waylaid at a saloon where she caused such a commotion that she was removed. Then she threw rocks through a plate glass window and was last seen being taken away in the city transfer wagon.[7] A jail sentence apparently served temporarily as a lesson for the culprit. In November Steers was given thirty days in the county jail, but no mention was made of his companion.[8]

Very likely Calamity had a past record for uproarious antics in Laramie, because when she returned there in 1887 a writer for the *Boomerang* said:

> To say that the old girl has reformed is somewhat of a chestnut. She was gloriously drunk this morning and if she didn't make Rome howl she did Laramie. Her resting place is now the soft side of an iron cell. Judge Pease will deliver the lecture and collect the fine in morning.[9]

Two weeks later this gentle creature turned up in the capital city of Wyoming in a very dilapidated condition. Though she apparently gave authorities no special trouble for awhile after her arrival, she was still remembered for her unbecoming conduct even after a decade away from the vicinity. The opening sentence of the notice about her return was that "after an absence of ten or eleven years, the notorious Calamity

---

[6] *Carbon County Journal,* September 18, 1886, citing *Meeker* (Colorado) *Herald.*
[7] *Carbon County Journal,* October 30, 1886.
[8] *Ibid.,* November 6, 1886.
Laramie (Wyoming) *Boomerang,* February 28, 1887.

Jane who used to figure so prominently in police courts and circles in this city, has again made her appearance in Cheyenne."[10]

A spicy charge was made against Calamity in Livingston, Montana, in the fall of 1888. The crime was fornication and the two guilty parties were Charles Townley and Jane Doe alias Calamity Jane. Bail was fixed at two hundred dollars and one hundred dollars respectively. The case was presented to the court on November 10, and the verdict came back from the jury "Not guilty."[11]

A year later back again in Wyoming, Calamity made herself at home in the Laramie jail. However, she was not the only woman making trouble for the law in that lively frontier town. The record shows that another female character spent a week's stretch there at the same time as Calamity Jane. It is interesting to imagine that the two were cellmates during their sojourn. A reporter noted briefly that:

> Two women, both well-known characters, were before Justice Tohren this morning charged with drunkenness. One was known as "Old Mother Gladdis," and the other as "Calamity Jane." They were given eight and a half days each and are now in jail.[12]

Having made contributions to the disruption of peace in Wyoming, Montana and Colorado, Calamity had no intention of slighting South Dakota. The day after she made her triumphant return to Deadwood in October, 1895, she paid a visit to the adjoining town of Lead. After patronizing a saloon she had to be bodily assisted into a hack by an officer to whom she used vile language.[13] Shortly after that she gave a drunken exhibi-

---

[10] *Democratic Leader* (Cheyenne, Wyoming), March 12, 1887.
[11] Papers are on file at Park County Courthouse, Livingston, Montana, in the Recorder's Office. Photostatic copies are found on pages 87 and 88.
[12] *Laramie Boomerang,* August 30, 1889.
[13] *Black Hills Daily Times* (Deadwood, South Dakota), October 6, 1895.

In the District Court

Of the Third Judicial District of the Territory of Montana.

IN AND FOR THE COUNTY OF PARK

TERRITORY OF MONTANA,
Plaintiff.

AGAINST

Charles Townley and
Jane Doe alias
Calamity Jane
Defendant

THE GRAND JURORS OF THE TERRITORY OF MONTANA, duly impaneled, sworn and charged at a stated term of the District Court aforesaid, begun and held at Livingston, within and for the County of Park aforesaid, Territory of Montana aforesaid, on the Fifth day of November A. D. one thousand eight hundred and eighty Eight to inquire in and for the County of Park aforesaid, upon their oath present that Charles Townley and Jane Doe alias Calamity Jane late of the County of Park aforesaid, on the first day of November A. D. one thousand eight hundred and Eight at the County of Park aforesaid did then and there commit the crime of Fornication in that the said Charles Townley an unmarried man and Jane Doe alias Calamity Jane an unmarried woman on said first day of November A.D. 1888 and on divers days times and occasions since the time last aforesaid at said County of Park aforesaid did willfully and unlawfully bed, cohabit and live together and have carnal knowledge of each other without then and there being married

Not Guilty

C. H. Crippens   Foreman

CONTRARY to the form of the statute in such case made and provided, and against the peace and dignity of the Territory of Montana

Allen R Joy

County Attorney of Park County, Montana Territory

by James G. Bailey *Deputy Clerk*

Thomas A. Farrell

to the _____ December, A.D. 1882

PRESENTED to the Court aforesaid in due _____

TERRITORY OF MONTANA

Charles Crawley and Jane Dr alias Calamity Jane Hunter

INDICTMENT FOR

A TRUE BILL

Dr. O Tabor
Foreman

WITNESSES

George W. Metcalf
John Sweeney
B.H. Campbell

Filed _____ $200.00

County Attorney of Park County Montana Territory

Allen R Joy

tion on the streets of Hot Springs. After attempting to take a ride on a saddle horse which did not belong to her, Calamity yelled revolting names to a young lady passing by, and had not a gentleman interfered it is possible she would have struck the lady. Although she carried on here in a high-handed, wild-west manner she was not arrested. However, the editor of the *Hot Springs Star* concluded in a disparaging paragraph about her conduct that "the disreputable outcast . . . should have been locked in the cooler."[14]

At the age of fifty, just a year before her death, Calamity still was experiencing that familiar sensation of sleeping in a cell. In the summer of 1902 she made an involuntary over night stop at the Livingston jail. The trouble all started when officials brought the old girl into Livingston to provide her with a berth at the county poorhouse. Her violent protests and promise to leave town brought release. Having a small amount of money she purchased a train ticket to Lombard, but missed the train and spent the layover drinking her favorite liquor. The station master, unable to put up with such a drunken nuisance, escorted her to the customary stronghold for the night.[15]

In Billings, however, she rated a sixty-day sentence as guest of the county on a charge of disturbing the peace. As she was in poor physical condition, the judge thought it a good idea to keep her away from temptation.[16] It could have been that she turned out to be more of a problem in jail than out, for twenty days later in a somewhat "jagged" condition she boarded a train for Deadwood.[17]

Without any authentication but repeated so often that it is often believed, there is a story of Calamity as a righteous thief. The story goes that, in Deadwood,

---

[14] *Ibid.*, November 14, 1895, citing *Hot Springs* (South Dakota) *Star.*
[15] *Livingston* (Montana) *Post,* June 5, 1902.
[16] *Billings* (Montana) *Gazette,* November 25, 1902.
[17] *Ibid.*, December 16, 1902.

Calamity worked in a questionable resort. One morning a particular patron, after awakening from his drunken slumbers, found that his thirty dollars were gone. Called before the justice of the peace to testify, Calamity readily admitted the theft. The man was completely drunk when she found him, so she ransacked his pocket for "loot" before the other girls could do likewise. When it was learned by the magistrate that she used the money to pay the hospital bill of a young girl without funds, the case was dropped and the gentleman reprimanded for his own unwise conduct.[18]

Captain Jack Crawford recalled that as assistant marshal of Custer City, South Dakota, in 1876 he was under the painful necessity of arresting Calamity for intoxication and disorderly conduct.[19]

Sometime in 1895, in Miles City, Mr. W. H. Newcom was asleep one night in the old stable office where he worked. The door opened and someone shook him. It was Calamity Jane. Booming out through the darkness that she wanted Newcom to take her to Deadwood, she told a tale of woe. Ed Jackson had put her in jail because she was a celebrity and Judge Milburn had fined her one hundred dollars. Since she had not had the money the judge had let her out to rustle it, but instead she was going to "make a run" for it. Promised that her friend, Sam Pepp, would pay for the trip, Newcom agreed to let her have a carriage and finally rounded up a driver. As the prisoner left Miles City, she shouted out that it had taken Jackson and two other men to put her in jail and that she would be back some day to get even with him.[20] Chances are that her escort dumped her off at the next town along the way where she could stay until her own fancy moved her or the law would take her in again.

[18] Jessie Brown and A. M. Willard, *The Black Hills Trails,* pp. 415-416.
[19] *Rapid City* (South Dakota) *Journal,* no date on clipping in file at South Dakota Historical Society Library. Context tells that it must have been a few weeks after Calamity Jane's death, August 1, 1903.
[20] *Miles City* (Montana) *Daily Star,* May 24, 1934.

These examples of Calamity Jane in jail were picked from only a few newspapers in the larger settlements. Careful and deliberate inspection of all local newspapers in towns where she visited would undoubtedly reveal dozens of similar news items. In addition, it is probable that for many misdemeanors she was not arrested and that in numerous places where she put in her appearance and was arrested the press failed to mention it. Her very nature indicates that her whole mature life was spent in and out of jails and that the above mentioned incidents are but a few that received extra publicity.

DRINKING WITH FRIENDS   Plate XXI

Calamity Jane liked to drink and she liked to do so in the company of
men. This convivial pose was taken at Gilt Edge, Mont., and the man
wearing her hat at a jaunty angle has been identified as Teddy Blue (E.
C.) Abbott, one of Montana's most colorful cowboys. The picture, said to
have been taken in about 1897 by Mrs. E. G. Worden of Lewistown, was
presented to the Historical Society of Montana in 1926. (See Picture Note
No. 2.)

Chapter XI.

THE GUNWOMAN

There is a group of tales about Calamity, which may very well have partial basis in fact, but which form a chapter in that great Western cycle which is still portrayed in moving picture thrillers. These are the tales about Calamity drawing her guns and outfacing an opponent or making him dance the tenderfoot dance[1] or otherwise do her bidding—the sort of thing which happens when the hero in the Hollywood western picture enters a saloon full of killers, dominating them with the strength of his reputation and a certain mystic quality which is part of the frontier mythology, or when he walks across a corral facing a barnful of armed desperadoes and manages to capture them. No one knows why he is not shot.

In a recent article on Wild Bill Hickok, Stewart Holbrook remarked that Wild Bill "made the town quiet and safe, and created a situation that was a marvel to all reflective men: here was the iron will of one man holding at bay all of the malice and lawlessness of a town that had been second to none in violence."[2]

In the mythology of the motion pictures, which goes back to the old dime-novels, this quality is usually connected with courage, will, a peculiar integrity, and a dominating eye. Since Calamity's eye, although described in a couple of instances as keen or piercing, was usually more accurately called bleary, and her reputation for integrity so dim, it is hard to think of her as being allowed to dominate on this basis. If cowboys and others danced at her bidding, it seems likely it was done as a kind of joke, to humor her. There is also the

---

[1] Tenderfoot dance was a frequent performance in which the gunman made his opponent dance by shooting close to his feet.

[2] Stewart H. Holbrook, "Wild Bill Hickok, There Was a Man," *Esquire,* May 1950, p. 64.

possibility, the last she would have cared to admit, that it depended somewhat on her being a woman. The frontiersman's confused chivalry and awe of women probably were not completely overcome even by Calamity's vehement rejection of the virtues of femininity. His code would have told him what to do when threatened by a man, but with a woman, even Calamity, he was baffled, and decided to enjoy it as a joke. California Joe, who actually was an Indian scout, was one man, however, who did not go along with this attitude. Milner, the nephew of California Joe, tells of a quarrel between Calamity and Joe when she allegedly tried to steal Joe's dog. It must be remembered that a scout's trained dog was a valuable piece of equipment. After that on two occasions Joe pulled his guns and made Calamity do the tenderfoot dance, as he said, to keep from being pestered any further by her.[3]

Although there are a few vague generalizations on Calamity as a killer of Indians or husbands, it is almost always stated that she was known not to be a killer. Therefore, this personality split becomes even wider. She was neither a reckless desperado nor a symbol of dominating integrity or righteousness. Nevertheless, she is credited with deeds appropriate only to one of these two types, or to an outstanding marksman, and there is no record of her marksmanship.

Here is a newspaper story of the tenderfoot *genre:*

This was in the cow town of Oakes, North Dakota. She drank much and in one saloon the cowboys began to chaff her. Calamity Jane smiled grimly and asked everyone up to the bar. They howled. Two revolvers suddenly appeared in the woman's hands. She could draw as quickly as any man who ever lived.

---

[3] Joe E. Milner and Earle R. Forrest, *California Joe,* p. 233.

"Dance, you tenderfeet, dance," she commanded grimly, and fired a few shots by way of emphasis. They danced, and with much vigor. They did other things that she commanded. Calamity Jane was not a person to be trifled with. The manner in which she shut up that saloon was powerfully convincing.[4]

Aikman reports that she was thrown out of a Livingston house of peculiarly riotous fame for the same performance, but not that she was interrupted in the act.[5] Later, he tells of her lining up a bunch of half-clad prostitutes and making them do the tenderfoot dance,[6] but to do so would hardly require any legendary courage.

Frackelton recounts how she terrified a newspaper editor in Sheridan, Wyoming, who wrote an offensive article about her.[7] There is another story of a visiting Chicago newspaperman hiding out in the Black Hills to avoid meeting her because he composed a bawdy lyric about her marital status.[8] An even more picturesque flight was executed by the city editor of the *Cheyenne Leader* who, when encountered by this particular female, "climbed upon a convenient desk, sprang through the skylight, ran nimbly across the adjacent roofs, jumped through another skylight and hid in a friend's office.[9] In these three cases the men may have wished only to avoid a scene, but that they are supposed to have made a quick exodus, instead of ignoring or dismissing Calamity, suggests that she had accumulated at least a reputation for impatience.

There is a story which shows Calamity in the role of the scourge against someone who is cruel to animals. The story appears in slightly different settings repeatedly. It is told in a *Literary Digest* article referring to

[4] *Avant Courier* (Bozeman, Montana), August 7, 1903.
[5] Duncan Aikman, *Calamity Jane and the Lady Wildcats*, p. 114.
[6] *Ibid.*, p. 121.
[7] Will Frackelton, *Sagebrush Dentist*, p. 124.
[8] *Anaconda Standard* (Butte, Montana), February 23, 1901.
[9] *Cheyenne* (Wyoming) *Daily Leader*, July 7, 1877.

a muleskinner whom Calamity found abusing a mule.[10] When she told him to stop, he flicked off her hat with his mulewhip. She pulled her guns and ordered him to put the hat back. "The mule skinner paused but a moment when he looked into the eyes confronting him, then picked up the hat and replaced it." In this case the muleskinner may not have been armed, and in any case had his hands full. But for the story to make sense he would have to be terrified that she would actually shoot. Another version of the story appears in Bennett's *Old Deadwood Days*:

> "Do you remember, Judge," the General said, "the time Calamity pulled a gun and a volley of language on a bull-whacker down here because he was belaboring a tired ox? He didn't even frown at the beast when she got through with him."[11]

Coursey recounts the story at greater length:

> An aged army officer gave this account of Jane, just after she died. He said that they were coming up the Black Hills' trail from Laramie to Deadwood with a pack train of army supplies. Jane was along. They had with them a new muleteer. He was an experienced driver, but had only recently been assigned to duty with the new command. Above Custer, along the creek, one of the mules went down. The fellow kicked it viciously with his heavy army boots and abused it mercilessly. Jane stood near, dressed as a government scout. The new driver did not know that she was a woman. Finally the Christian instincts in Jane's heart got the better of her, and stepping up to the villain she said: "Don't you kick that mule again!" With that he gave a sharp flirt with his whip, and jerked her hat to the ground.

---

[10] "Calamity Jane as a Lady Robinhood," *Literary Digest*, November 14, 1925, p. 48.
[11] Estelline Bennett, *Old Deadwood Days,* p. 239.

Quicker than a flash, Calamity Jane jerked out her big Colt's revolver, stuck the muzzle firmly under his nose and commanded: "Put that hat where you got it!"

He saw the white circle forming rapidly around her firm mouth, and judging by the look in her eyes and the tone of her voice, he promptly obeyed.

She said: "Thank you," and walked away.[12]

Tom Brown gives an eye-witness account of Calamity Jane's appearing in a grocery store in Confederate Gulch in 1866, getting a sack of groceries including items that were luxurious in that day, then pulling her guns and backing out without the grocer's daring to interfere.[13] The motive for this action was the need to feed her patients who were ill in a nearby cabin. If the story were true it seems like a deliberate effort to show off. With the open-handed generosity of the frontier, it would have been simple to take up a collection for the afflicted. The story, however, appears in another form in Deadwood:

During one of these epidemics, her epic has it, a new store proprietor sold a hard looking female an assortment of groceries and preserved delicacies that would have kept a fair-sized family through a Montana winter. He helped her wedge her treasures into a capacious burlap sack and throw it over her sturdy shoulders. Then he bent over his counter to make the addition. When he looked up he was facing down the muzzle of a steadily pointed six-shooter and a sinister contralto thunder was rolling about his ears.

"I'm Calamity Jane, by God, and them sick boys I'm lookin' out for up in the hills don't pay for no grub till they get good and able. Get that?" As

---

[12] O. S. Coursey, *Beautiful Black Hills*, pp. 105-107.
[13] Tom Brown, *The Romance of Everyday Life*, pp. 41-42.

she vanished through the door with the approved
backing-out step of the successful stick-up artists,
amused by-standers convinced him that to attempt
prosecution under the circumstances would be a
dangerously anti-social manoeuvre.[14]

An article written by Glendolin Wagner tells the same
story with this stirring conclusion: "the weak-kneed
proprietor never even gasped out his protest, for he
knew that a leveled gun in Calamity's ever steady hand,
backed by the steady glint of hard eyes, meant business."[15]

Another story turns up frequently, that of the bartender who refused to give her drink because ladies
were not allowed in bars in those days. As told by Aikman it goes like this:

> . . . a new bartender in the town, with the re-
> straints of Denver's drinking proprieties firmly en-
> grained in his nature, declined to give her service.
> He found himself looking into the barrel of her
> pistol and heard a hearty contralto voice command-
> ing, "I reckon you don't know who I am. Say, young
> feller, don't you know if Calamity Jane wasn't a
> lady, you might be setting up drinks right now for
> this blankety-blank crowd?" A bystander inter-
> posed at this point with a sufficient explanation.
> Also, as was often characteristic of her patronage, he
> paid for her drink.[16]

Calamity herself started a lurid story about how she
overpowered Jack McCall, the murderer of Wild Bill
Hickok. This time she used a meat cleaver.

---

[14] Duncan Aikman, p. 107.

[15] Glendolin Damon Wagner, "Calamity Jane," *Montana Oil and Mining
Journal,* January 1936, p. 7.

[16] Duncan Aikman, pp. 57-58.

On the 2nd of August, while setting at a gambling table in the Bell Union saloon, in Deadwood, he [Wild Bill] was shot in the back of the head by the notorious Jack McCall, a desperado. I was in Deadwood at the time and on hearing of the killing made my way at once to the scene of the shooting and found that my friend had been killed by Mc-Call. I at once started to look for the assassin and found him at Shurdy's butcher shop and grabbed a meat cleaver and made him throw up his hands; through the excitement on hearing of Bill's death, having left my weapons on the post of my bed. He was then taken to a log cabin and locked up, well secured as every one thought, but he got away and was afterwards caught at Fagan's ranch on Horse Creek, on the old Cheyenne road and was then taken to Yankton, Dak., where he was tried, sentenced and hung.[17]

The *Pioneer* related only that "Jack McCall was captured after a lively chase by many of the citizens."[18] McClintock, who was on the street when McCall ran from the saloon, said that the assassin "was found by Ike Brown and others." He added that "no report was current at that time of him resisting arrest nor were there 'ten men armed with rifles' making the arrest."[19] Because of these reports the only conclusion that can be drawn is that the autobiographer was not telling the truth about her part in the drama. If Calamity went into the Belle Union Saloon to find the murdered Wild Bill, she must have been sadly disappointed. His corpse, according to the same news item mentioned above, was not there, but at the hall of Nuttall and Mann. The Belle Union was much farther down the street, but certainly no one would criticize her for confusing a saloon or two.

[17] *Autobiography,* pp. 4-5.
[18] Jessie Brown and A. M. Willard, *The Black Hills Trails,* p. 407, citing the *Pioneer* (Deadwood, South Dakota) August 5, 1876.
[19] John S. McClintock, *Pioneer Days in the Black Hills,* pp. 108-109.

Mokler and Cunningham give her credit for the capture.[20] Nelson seems to relate the incident in earnest, although he scoffs at a good many of her other claims. He may have assumed that the reader would recognize his sarcasm.[21] Connelley makes quite a point of the story, adding the element that the timorous men around at the time were afraid to go after McCall in his hideaway, but that Calamity stalked in, unarmed and captured him with the cleaver.[22] Why McCall, who had just shot Wild Bill with no qualms, would not have shot her too is beyond interpretation. It should be remembered that these men are but recent writers and that they took their opinion from her story.

A brave deed often retold shows the daring and courage of Calamity Jane in rescuing a Cheyenne and Black Hills stage. There are writers who tell the story exactly as she narrated it and believe it, others who claim the story may be partially sound and still others who call the whole thing ridiculous. Her own thrilling version reads:

> I remained around Deadwood locating claims, going from camp to camp until the spring of 1877, where one morning, I saddled my horse and rode towards Crook city. I had gone about twelve miles from Deadwood, at the mouth of Whitewood creek, when I met the overland mail running from Cheyenne to Deadwood. The horses on a run, about two hundred yards from the station; upon looking closely I saw they were pursued by Indians. The horses ran to the barn as was their custom. As the horses stopped I rode along side of the coach and found the driver John Slaughter, lying face downwards in the boot of the stage, he having been shot by the Indians. When the stage got to the station the Indians hid

[20] Alfred James Mokler, *History of Natrona County Wyoming,* 1888-1922, p. 433.

[21] Bruce O. Nelson, *Land of the Dacotahs,* p. 164.

[22] William Elsey Connelley, *Wild Bill and His Era.* p. 191.

in the bushes. I immediately removed all baggage from the coach except the mail. I then took the driver's seat and with all haste drove to Deadwood, carrying the six passengers and the dead driver.[23]

The tale could be accepted as fact except for newspaper accounts written at the time of the incident. Since there are no Deadwood files available until July, 1877, and the murder occurred in March, 1877, the account in the Cheyenne, Wyoming, daily, taken from some Deadwood journals, is adequate to settle the points in question. The newspaper narrative relates:

Deadwood City, March 26.

A bold attempt to rob the Cheyenne & Black Hills stage, bound north, was made near here last evening. As the coach was coming down Whitewood canyon and about two and a half miles from Deadwood, five masked men, walking along the road before the stage, suddenly wheeled, ordered the driver to stop and instantly commenced firing on the coach. At the first fire Johnny Slaughter, the driver was killed and Walker Iler of Deadwood, was slightly wounded in the hand and arm. The horses started suddenly, throwing the driver, Iler and another passenger off the coach. The stage was not stopped until it arrived in town, leaving the driver on the road dead. About twenty shots were fired at the coach, but all the passengers, except Iler, were unhurt. A party went out and found the body of the driver with a charge of buckshot in his breast. The robbers got no booty.[24]

. . . had it not been for the stage team taking fright and running away, in all probability the ten passengers would have shared a like fate with the driver.[25]

[23] *Autobiography*, p. 5.
[24] *Cheyenne* (Wyoming) *Daily Sun*, March 27, 1877.
[25] *Ibid.*, March 30, 1877.

The fact that Calamity's name was not mentioned
in the article is ample proof that she had no part in the
affair. Calamity, whose name was becoming a household word and who had her name appearing in newspapers all over the West, would certainly have rated a
few lines telling of the daring rescue, had she actually
effected it. It is obvious why it did not appear. She
was not there. The discrepancies in her story are so
numerous as to provoke amusement. Here is how the
two stories compare point for point:

Calamity	*Newspaper*
1 One morning.	Last evening.
2 About twelve miles from Dead-wood.	About two and a half miles from Deadwood.
3 I saw they were pursued by In-dians.	Five masked men, walking along the road from the stage, suddenly wheeled.
4 The six passengers.	The ten passengers
5 Found the driver . . . lying face downwards in the boot of the stage . . . and drove to Dead-wood, carrying . . . the dead driver.	Leaving the driver on the road dead . . . A party went out and found the body of the driver.

The comparison proves beyond doubt that Calamity
Jane was not at the spot when the hold-up took place.
The woman probably was not even in town to read
the newspapers. She must have gotten the story second-
or third-hand and then later made it her own.

Investigation at the scene of Calamity's activities produced a tale which may be authentic. If it is, it shows
that even in her later period, people felt they could
count on her in time of need. William Berry, an eighty-
four year old Missoula resident, for a number of years
related this story which reeks of the Old West.[26]

Between 1895 and 1902 Mr. Berry was a passenger
conductor on the Northern Pacific Railway in south
central Montana. Calamity Jane was often a passenger
on his run and they were casual friends for several
years. One night Calamity boarded the train at Billings

---

[26] Interview with Mr. William Berry July 1949.

BILLINGS IN 1880's

This picture, taken in the 1880's, shows the main street of Billings during a street parade. This was one of many Montana towns which Calamity Jane frequented, usually riotously, during her lifetime. Historical Society of Montana photo.

Plate XXII

enroute to Bozeman. As was her usual custom, she sat in the front part of the smoking car. Forty miles out of Billings at the little town of Columbus, Sam Jackson, under-sheriff of Sweet Grass County, got on the train and confided to Berry that he had warrants for the arrest of two cattle rustlers whom he spied in the back of the smoking car. Unable to make the arrest there in Columbus because the town possessed no jail, Jackson had conceived a workable plan. They were to proceed up the line to Big Timber, where officers from that town had been notified of the situation and were to meet the train to help with the final disposition of the ruffians. Berry was to lock the front door so that all the passengers getting off would have to file past the sheriff. Then Jackson saw Calamity and nudged Berry: "Say, Bill, as you go through the smoker casually tell Calamity to amble back this way. I have a hunch that besides those two scoundrels there may be an accomplice or two sitting somewhere in the car. In case that is true, I will probably need some help from her." Bill passed on the message and she played her part with aplomb. In ten or fifteen minutes she swaggered out to the under-sheriff and received instructions. After coming back to her seat she took a nap. She had her reliable six-shooter and that was all she needed. It was always kept in a holster under her left arm beneath a buckskin coat or jacket. As the train neared Big Timber, Bill Berry locked the front door and called the station. He requested those getting off to exit through the back. The train stopped, Jackson showed his badge, poked his gun at the two rustlers who obligingly forfeited theirs, and made the arrest. The sheriff's suspicion had been right: there was an accomplice sitting a few seats from his two friends who started to come to their rescue while Jackson was handcuffing his victims. As the third man made his first sudden move for his gun, Calamity quickly and quietly stepped from behind and stuck her gun against his back. "Drop that gun, brother, right on the seat." He did. By that time she had changed her expression from that of grim determination to a wide smile. "Here, sheriff, is another gun for your collection," she added.

In the memoirs of D. Dee there is a passage which indicates that many of Calamity's gun performances were mock serious:

> "When Calamity decided it was time to go on another spree, her first idea was to don her buckskin suit, high-heeled boots, and Stetson hat, a wide ammunition belt and 2 44's holstered at each side. She looked like a very formidable person and anyone who crossed her got cussed up one side and down the other, and she was a past master at profanity. I never knew her to fight with her fists, but when in a peevish fit, out came one or both of her big 44's and folks were told where to head in. She was never known to be a killer, but one didn't know but what now was the time she would start in, and the big bores of her 44's aiming at the midsection was an excellent persuader. 'All right, Jane, I'll take it all back,' would mollify her and a drink made her forget any differences in a second."[27]

A few years after her death an acquaintance of Calamity Jane reminisced: "But she was a kind-hearted girl; there wasn't anything vicious about her, either. She never got into fights or wanted to pull a gun, or anything like that."[28]

---

[27] D. Dee, *Low Down on Calamity Jane*, pp. 6-7.
[28] *Great Falls* (Montana) *Leader*, July 16, 1906.

Chapter XII.

DEATH

After the turn of the century, Calamity Jane's seemingly rugged health began to fail. Her friends noticed that she was not as robust as she once had been.[1] Her boisterous past was catching up with her.

If she herself realized this she did not show it, for early in 1903 Calamity went back to her old haunts in the Black Hills country. Travelling from town to town and camp to camp, she renewed acquaintances with her old pioneer friends and sold her little *Autobiography* and scouting pictures. Her life was a gay one and seemed to be made up of one drunken carousal after another. An amusing incident took place as she rode in a hack from Aladdin to Sun Dance, Wyoming. The episode was of a more temperate nature than many in which she had figured, but it illustrates the personality and character of this frontier woman, then in her early fifties. Riding across the hills she yelled at everyone she met, asking for a drink of whisky or a smoke. She passed two fellows herding horses who were sitting on the ground playing cards. "High, low, Jack and the game," she shouted. "Got a bottle?" When they informed her that they had no bottle she asked for a smoke. Their negative reply brought a request for a chew. One of the men produced a plug of Climax and she took a chew "that would have made a Kentuckian ashamed of himself."[2] That was Calamity Jane as she neared the end of the trail.

Early in July of 1903 she spent some time in Deadwood and on one occasion expressed a desire to re-visit the grave of Wild Bill Hickok. A prominent man, Percy Russell, who lived until 1957, hired "Wim's Hack" for her and the two went up to Mt. Moriah Cemetery. At-

---

[1] *Pioneer-Times* (Deadwood, South Dakota), July 15, 1903.
[2] *Ibid.*, June 25, 1903.

tired in a long black dress and broad brimmed hat, Calamity posed for a picture by Hickok's grave.[3] This photograph has long been used on post cards sold each year to tourists.

For the next few weeks the movements of this wandering woman are uncertain, but in the last week of July she went from Spearfish to Terry, a small mining town eight miles southwest of Deadwood.[4] Complaining that she was sick and weary, Calamity Jane told friends that her time was near to "cash in." There, in Terry, she was cared for by Mr. H. A. Sheffer, proprietor of the Calloway Hotel. Her characteristic spirit was displayed in her reception of the attention of her physician. She showed a rebellious disposition when her doctor tried to give her medicine. Luckily for Dr. Richards, her weakened physical condition kept her from carrying out numerous threats. The day before her death the editor of the Terry *News-Record* visited Deadwood to solicit aid for this impoverished old woman from members of the Black Hills Pioneer Society. Several old friends called on her at the hotel where she was staying. To them she spoke of a married daughter living in North Dakota, but would not reveal any details about how she was getting along or why the two had quarreled. Her "dying request" was that the funeral to be held under the auspices of the Pioneers. She wanted her remains to be buried in Mt. Moriah Cemetery in Deadwood beside those of Wild Bill who was murdered twenty-seven years before in Deadwood. Her demise occurred at five o'clock in the afternoon of August 1, 1903. The immediate cause of her death was recorded by the doctor and undertaker as inflamma-

---

[3] Interview with Percy Russell July 1949.

The same idea appears in a short unpublished paper in possession of Mr. Russell, *Calamity Jane as Remembered by Percy Russell.* (Editor's note: See Picture Note 4 concerning picture which appears following page 108.)

[4] Most accounts state that Calamity died in Terraville, South Dakota. It is a town less than a mile from Deadwood.

Calamity Jane

THE AILING CALAMITY   Plate XXIII

Calamity Jane's health was rapidly deteriorating when this picture was taken in Whitewood, S. Dak. in the summer of 1903. The photographer was Charles Haas of Deadwood, S. Dak. Haas' story of how this picture happened to be taken is found in Picture Note No. 3 in the back of the book. Reproduced through courtesy of J. Leonard Jennewein, Mitchell, S. Dak.

tion of the bowels,[5] but over indulgence in alcohol over a period of many years was undoubtedly a contributing cause.

The body was brought to the undertaking parlors of Charles Robinson in Deadwood. Calamity had taken care of Robinson one winter when the boy was only seven years old and throughout the years a sort of friendship had continued.[6] While she lay on the cooling board, many curious women, who would have scorned her on the street, came to look at the face of the dead woman. They clipped locks of her hair for souvenirs, and so disgusted was a former crony of hers with their vandal-like actions that he had a wire screen put over her head.[7]

Her friends who gathered to see her agreed that she looked better than she had ever looked in her lifetime. A photograph taken of her in the coffin shows her serene and neat. The white dress was very different from the buckskin outfits or plain black dresses which earlier pictures show as her ordinary costume. According to the Diamond Jubilee Edition of the *Pioneer-Times*, Mrs. Gilbert Parker, the only lady from the days of '76 still living in Deadwood, claimed that she made the dress in which Calamity was buried.[8] This is extremely doubtful. A newspaper article thirteen years

---

[5] *Pioneer-Times*, August 2, 1903.

This writer was able to unearth a book which contained the records of deaths in early Deadwood. It is of special value because the county records did not begin until considerably later. Vital information about Calamity was written in and signed by both the doctor and undertaker. That data should end any and all controversy concerning her death over which writers disagree.

[6] In an interview July 1949 with Mrs. Mary Robinson, widow of undertaker Charles Robinson. She told that when her husband's mother had to go East one winter to a funeral Calamity took little Charles to the shack where she lived. He needed additional winter clothing so she made him a pair of trousers from a red California blanket. Several times over a period of years she did services for this family and they never forgot her. In later years, Mr. Robinson gave financial aid whenever she needed it but he insisted that she never come to his home. Despite her kindness, he realized that she was not a fit associate for his wife and children.

[7] Jesse Brown and A. M. Willard, *The Black Hills Trails*, p. 418.

[8] *Pioneer-Times*, June 20, 1951.

earlier carried a story in which Mrs. Parker said that "the famous frontiers-woman was buried in a plain black dress, with a white collar." The claim of the seamstress is in contradiction to the photograph which shows Calamity in white. In the earlier interview Mrs. Parker did not claim that she had made the dress, as she surely would have done had she taken such a part in the funeral of the notorious woman.[9]

To this day Deadwood has seldom seen such a funeral. The services were held in the First Methodist Church on August 4, and the building was packed with old settlers as well as many morbidly curious citizens. Dr. C. B. Clark delivered the sermon and Mrs. M. M. Wheeler and Miss Elsie Cornwall sang, accompanied at the organ by Miss Helen Fowler. After reading the Ninetieth Psalm and making a few remarks upon the uncertainty of life and the level to which death brings everyone, the Reverend Dr. Clark reviewed the history of Deadwood and the part which Calamity Jane had played in its development. He stressed the kindness she had exhibited and recalled her part in nursing the sick during several epidemics. The more unpleasant and sordid things were tactfully omitted. At the close of the sermon the remains were viewed by several hundred persons.[10] Mrs. Parker in her estimate that "over ten thousand people crowded around the Methodist Church" was exaggerating grossly.[11]

As the people filed out of the church they noticed that a man who had been attracting their attention by his weeping and wailing throughout the service was still kneeling and sobbing bitterly. No one knew him, but some one touched him on the shoulder and asked if he were a friend of Calamity Jane. "Yes," he said between sobs, "I was her first husband. She was the finest

---

[9] *Great Falls* (Montana) *Tribune,* November 19, 1938. (United Press Dispatch from Deadwood November 19.)

[10] *Deadwood Daily Pioneer-Times,* August 5, 1903.

[11] Great Falls Tribune, November 19, 1938. (United Press Dispatch from Deadwood, November 19.)

AT WILD BILL'S GRAVE   Plate XXIV

This is one of the last pictures taken of Calamity Jane alive. The scene was the grave of Wild Bill Hickok at Mt. Moriah Cemetery in Deadwood in the late summer of 1903. Calamity died a short time later and was buried near where she is standing. Picture Note No. 4 in the back of this book contains more detailed material about the occasion on which this and possibly other pictures were taken.

woman that ever lived—the kindest."[12] Sons and daughters of the Pioneers still remember that incident as told by their parents in after years. One lady laughingly said that her mother recalled a remark by Seth Bullock on the subject of the stricken spouse: "The Methodist Church could never possibly house all of Calamity Jane's so-called husbands."[13] While no one was interested enough at the time to find out more about this man, they assumed that he was some imposter trying to get a few dollars from the Pioneers. He did, and was never seen again.[14]

Calamity was conveyed in the hearse down Lee Street and up to Mt. Moriah Cemetery. She was escorted by many of the old settlers and the band which always came out in full dress for such an occasion. The road leading to the cemetery winds around and up some five hundred feet above the town. The grade is so sharply steep that tourists often ask how Deadwood buries its dead there in the icy winter.

In compliance with her dying request, she was deposited beside Wild Bill Hickok after a brief ceremony. Of the five pall-bearers one, George S. Hopkins, was still living in 1950, a bartender in a popular tavern. The Old Pioneers provided a handsome casket and purchased the desired burial lot. Sympathetic friends sent masses of floral offerings that all but concealed the casket.[15] The tombstone which today marks her grave is a small simple stone slab with the inscription:

CALAMITY JANE

MRS. M. E. BURKE

DIED AUG. 1, 1903

AGED 53 YEARS

---

[12] Estelline Bennett, *Old Deadwood Days,* p. 243.
[13] Seth Bullock was the first sheriff of Deadwood, U. S. marshal, Rough Rider and intimate friend of Theodore Roosevelt, and one of Deadwood's most outstanding citizens in the early days.
[14] Miss Florence Rankin told this story in the public library one day in Deadwood. She knew no other stories although she said her mother used to tell lots of them when the children were much younger.
[15] *Deadwood Daily Pioneer-Times,* August 2 and 8, 1903.

Something like a fable has grown up around the date of Calamity Jane's death. It rivals almost any of the stories about the date of her birth. From the fact that she died on August 1, 1903, and Wild Bill died on August 2, 1876, some writers insisted that Calamity passed away on the anniversary of Wild Bill's death. Typical of the stories giving the date of her death, is one by O. W. Coursey, historian and one-time poet laureate of South Dakota: "By a strange hand of fate, the Judge of the Universe called her before the bar of omnipotent justice on the same day of the month, twenty-seven years later, that her consort Wild Bill, beside of whom she requested to be buried, met his death."[16] Another writer gives the whole affair an even more mystic touch when he says that "she passed away on August 2, 1906. On the same day and month and same hour Wild Bill was assassinated thirty years before."[17]

There is no more truth in such stories about the time of her death than in many of the fabrications which have been woven around the life of this strange woman. Of all the half-legendary characters who roamed the frontier in the last quarter of the nineteenth century and whose exploits have provoked the imagination, one of the most amazing was Calamity Jane.

---

[16] *Sioux Falls* (South Dakota) Argus Leader, August 30, 1924.
[17] Harry "Sam" Young *Hard Knocks*, p. 206.
   Young is historically off three years in the date of her death.

Calamity Jane August 1ʰⁱ" 1903

CALAMITY JANE AT PEACE   Plate **XXV**

This picture of Calamity Jane in her coffin is the only one of its kind known to exist. The original is in possession of the author of this book, and any reproduction of it is forbidden. The pure white dress in which this strange woman was dressed for burial was in sharp contrast to the rough mannish garb she wore in life. Picture Note 5 at the back of the book contains further information about this picture.

THE GRAVE AT MT. MORIAH   Plate XXVI

This is Calamity Jane's grave at Mt. Moriah Cemetery in Deadwood. The body of Wild Bill Hickok, who was killed in 1876, was disinterred from its grave in Inglewood and reburied in this cemetery. Calamity Jane is said to have muttered on her deathbed that she wished to be buried beside Hickok, and this was done. Whether or not there was any real romance or marriage between these two frontier characters, they share common ground in Deadwood. Photo by J. Leonard Jennewein, Mitchell, S. Dak.

EPILOGUE

A COMPILATION OF OPINIONS ABOUT AND ATTITUDES TOWARD CALAMITY JANE

GENERAL:

In all the existing material written about Calamity Jane there is a remarkable hesitation to condemn her, in spite of the fact that her sexual irregularities and drunken escapades were prodigious and well-known. The material includes the memoirs of a lady of unimpeachable character, as well as those of a renowned madame, and accounts by journalists, historians, a government official of long service, and a number of pioneers who knew Calamity Jane. Yet in all this array of accounts there is little of protest or indignation about her uproarious activities, particularly during the early years of her career when she and a few prostitutes were the only women in the region.

A few, however, criticized Calamity for her riotous conduct and attacked those who defended her. In a letter to the *Deadwood Champion* in 1877 one indignant Deadwood citizen bitterly upbraided that newspaper's editor for attempting to dignify Calamity as a frontier heroine. The letter had little effect upon the editor, apparently, for three months later he was hailing his heroine as "beginning to take front rank amongst the few famous ladies in the [Black] Hills."[1]

A generation later attitudes were changing with the movement of wives and families to the Black Hills and the shift of the frontier westward. Former boom-towns were taking on an air of respectability as the century drew to a close. To a few old-timers Calamity Jane may have epitomized "the good old days," but to staid newcomers who demanded peace and quiet, she was becom-

---

[1] *Deadwood* (South Dakota) *Champion,* December 2, 1877.

111

ing a nuisance. When the *Black Hills Daily Times* brought out a laudatory editorial about Calamity upon her return to Deadwood, outraged citizens wrote indignantly to the editor. The newspaper reacted quickly to this popular pressure, and atoned for its indiscretion by referring to Calamity as "a notorious ruin."[2]

Most of the writers who have dealt with Calamity Jane have written long after the fact, and few have given precise indications of their sources. But there is usually a vague evidence that contacts were made with people who had known her or known of her. Thus the vast variety of stories and opinions about her, although difficult to assay for fact, at least adds up to a report of a general attitude toward her. There are some ringing denunciations of her behavior, but few that show evidence of reflecting contemporary opinion. In the case of those writers who actually knew her, there is an even greater tendency to point out her rough virtues as outweighing her obvious vices.

Calamity Jane's violent personality certainly contained some characteristics that endeared her to the rough and ready companions of the early boom days. Her spasmodic generosity; her brusque, rough sympathy for the underdog; her failure to be impressed with riches, fine clothes or "society;" her lack of pretense or affectation of virtue; her complete rejection of simpering femininity; such attributes were esteemed on the frontier. She was a symbol of rough virtue—hardiness with a heart of gold and a lively sense of humor. She completely ignored high society's condemnation of unconventional frontier ways. Few who were anywhere near the scene of her activities were in the least deceived about her status as a kind of eccentric prostitute. Nowhere in the record is there approval of her aberrations but there is much support for the view that her virtues outweighed her vices.

---

[2] *Black Hills* (Deadwood, South Dakota) *Daily Times,* November 14, 1895.

The following sections of this chapter will deal with the attitudes which lay behind the hesitation to condemn her and will attempt to establish her relation to frontier society as a person and as a legend. There will be little emphasis on the authenticity of the various sources, since in most cases the evidence is vague, and since the material is being considered as a record of opinion, rather than for its value as historical evidence.

HEART-OF-GOLD-VINDICATION:

Most of the many commentators who have good words to say for Calamity take the attitude that under her rough exterior was a "heart of gold" which led her to many good deeds that more than outweighed her scandalous conduct. From the point of view of her early rough-living companions, this might have served as a justification for themselves, and a general vindication for the outcast status of frontier society in some quarters. The same attitude, however, shows up elsewhere.

For instance, in the book called *McGillycuddy Agent,* Julia McGillycuddy, second wife of a physician and topographer who said he knew Calamity Jane in 1875, records her husband's views in a book on his life which he dictated. McGillycuddy after this period was a government official for many years, and would be expected to represent a typical bourgeois point of view. Nevertheless, as he tells the story according to his second wife's reporting it, he and his first wife were completely aware of Calamity Jane's whoring, drunkenness, and general scandalous behavior, but knew no one who cared to condemn her. McGillycuddy recounts seeing Calamity Jane's drunken offer to care for a boy stricken with smallpox after the return of General Crook's starved army in 1876, and his wife reports his reaction to it as follows:

> Then the Doctor recalled incidents of his former acquaintance with Calamity. He spoke of her kindness to anyone in trouble, as well as her utter reck-

lessness and lack of morals, expressing his opinion
that there was much more real feelings in the hearts
of the average rough human beings of the West
than in those of more cultured centers.[3]

In a letter written in 1924 to the editor of the *Rapid City
Journal,* McGillycuddy showed the same attitude:

> Jane was a healthy girl of an affectionate dis-
> position, and naturally had many husbands, license
> shops and preachers being scarce in those days, she
> would select a new one when occasion made it desir-
> able or necessity required. She was not immoral, she
> was unmoral, she lived in accordance with the light
> given her, and the conditions and the times.[4]

Those two quotations indicate a consistent opinion of
Calamity Jane's character from the same man. The book
was published in 1941, three years after McGillycuddy's
death and seventeen years after the letter to the Journal. He had had plenty of time to reconstruct his view
or forget the past as it really was. Yet, he held to his
earlier attitude.

Miss Estelline Bennett, a most highly esteemed Deadwood citizen, would be expected to reflect a conventional point of view. When a youngster she looked upon
Calamity Jane as something like Alice in Wonderland
or Joan of Arc. That childish view would be of little
importance if it did not surely reflect adult attitudes,
in all likelihood somewhat tempered for children's ears.
Many years later when writing her book, *Old Deadwood Days,* Miss Bennett still spoke respectfully of
Calamity Jane.

Her father and uncle, Judge Bennett and General
Dawson, both regarded Calamity as a prostitute, but
still they had good words for her character, generosity

---

[3] Julia B. McGillycuddy, *McGillycuddy Agent,* pp. 72-73.

[4] In a letter from McGillycuddy to the editor of the *Rapid City* (South Dakota) *Journal* dated October 1, 1924 on file at the South Dakota Historical Society Library (Pierre).

and charity. In fact, it was the general who introduced his niece to Calamity on the streets of Deadwood in 1895.[5]

Brown and Willard, presumably reflecting the opinions of old-timers, many of whom were around when their book was written, summarize the general attitude as follows:

> She was a strange mixture of the wild, untamed character of the plains and mountain trails, and generous kindly womanhood. But under the rough exterior there beat a heart so big and friendly as to be without measure. Brave, energetic, unfettered, kind, always on the line of action, with helping hand ever turned to the poor and unfortunate, the personality of Calamity Jane became indelibly stamped upon the minds of the pioneers.[6]

Frackelton tells of an old mule-skinner, who had what the author describes as a "confused attitude" toward Calamity. He speaks of a family feeling between the people who shared the frontier's rough unconventionality, and a feeling of disloyalty in speaking ill of such a one.

> I worked with Jane on three freight trips with a bull string. She took her place as any man would, and did her share of the work with the best of them. But when night came, if any of the boys wanted to go to the brush, she was always willin' to pull off a pants leg.

Then the old mule skinner paused and said reflectively, "Doc, just forget I said that. Jane was a perfect angel sent from heaven when any of the boys was sick, and gave them a mother's care till they got well."[7]

Captain Jack Crawford, who was chief of U. S. Army scouts in Calamity's time, states definitely that she was

[5] Estelline Bennett, *Old Deadwood Days,* p. 220.

[6] Jessie Brown and A. M. Willard, *The Black Hills Trails,* p. 417.

[7] Will Frackelton, *Sagebrush Dentist,* p. 125.

never a scout, stagedriver, or express messenger, as she claimed in her *Autobiography*. But he adds, "It is to her credit that she did retain a kind generous heart, even while following in the footsteps of her dissolute father and careless mother."[8]

Otero, former governor of New Mexico, who probably had only hearsay knowledge of Calamity Jane although he claims to have seen her personally, gives her the same reputation: "She was typical of those unfortunate women of the frontier in her charity, and willingness to spend their last dollar to aid anyone in distress."[9]

In 1895, on her return to Deadwood after an absence of sixteen years, the *Black Hills Daily Times* gave her a hearty welcome and the following review of her reputation:

> She did not wait for an introduction, but reached out her hand for a friendly grasp and was glad to see us. This is her disposition. She has always been known for her friendliness, generosity, and happy cordial manner. It didn't matter to her whether a person was rich or poor, white or black, or what their circumstances were, Calamity Jane was just the same to all. Her purse was always open to help a hungry fellow, and she was one of the first to proffer her help in cases of sickness, accidents, or any distress.[10]

Wilstach, who in general was most eager to discount all talk of her romance with his hero, Wild Bill Hickok, nevertheless admits that "she lived a hard and vicious life, yet she had a most kind and generous heart."[11]

D. Dee, pseudonym for a famous madame at Belle Fourche and Rapid City, South Dakota, who knew Calamity Jane, explains in her discreet memoirs what Jane's status was in the frontier community. She puts

---

[8] *Rapid City* (South Dakota) *Journal*, no date on clipping in files South Dakota Historical Society Library. Context tells that it must have been a few weeks after Calamity Jane's death, August 1, 1903.

[9] Miguel Otero, *My Life on the Frontier*, p. 22.

[10] *Black Hills Daily Times*, October 5, 1895.

[11] Frank J. Wilstach, *Wild Bill Hickok*, p. 263.

it gently, perhaps aware that it was absurd that she should feel called upon to apologize for one whose escapades exceeded those of her own employees only in the publicity they received:

> As an old-timer said, "Jane had a very affectionate nature." There were very few preachers around to bother, so whenever she got tired of one man she soon selected a new one. But deeds, not morals, were needed in those days, and many can testify to the many good deeds she did.[12]

George Hoshier was an old friend of Calamity Jane. In reminiscing about her and her friends, Madame Moustache and Stem-Winder, female card-dealers, he was quoted as follows:

> Those were all good-natured, kind women. Of course none of them would jump out like Calamity. She was always there first. It didn't make any difference what was the matter with a person, if Calamity could help them she would. She was the girl who went to Elizabethtown, here in Deadwood, and took care of a man. He was a stranger to her and had the smallpox. Nobody else would go near him, and she went and took care of him and brought him through all right. She was a fine nurse.[13]

In the collections of material compiled by the South Dakota Department of History there is a summary of the characteristics that established the legendary Calamity Jane, as well as the real person, in the affections of many early settlers:

> One of the best known characters who was conspicuous in the early history of the Hills was a woman known far and wide as Calamity Jane. She was a series of paradoxes. She was three persons in one. She was a type of the Hills, she was three types

---

[12] D. Dee, *Low Down on Calamity Jane*, p. 3.
[13] *Great Falls* (Montana) *Leader*, July 16, 1906.

in one. The first was that of a common camp follower, lewd, disgusting—a menace to society. She also represented another type of the carefree, independent and unruly character that haunted the border. She was a reckless horsewoman, a crack shot, fearless and adventurous, never known to abandon a friend in a fight. She loved the wild free life of the West; she hated the conventions of fine society. She was a tomboy frontiersman. In one respect she represented a distinct type of the early settler for she had much of the milk of human kindness in her nature. Her deeds of charity and benevolence have therefore rescued her from oblivion and the odium that the world is wont to heap upon women that succumb to her vices.[14]

AS A SYMBOL OF THE GOOD OLD DAYS:

Although it does not match the great chorus of opinions which holds that Calamity's rough frontier virtues outweighed her vices, there is still a numerous group of comments which attempts to make her represent something special which only old-timers could understand and which could not be appreciated in a later day of vanishing virility. She became a symbol of the nostalgia of an exclusive group who shared the knowledge of the special circumstances of boomtown barbarity and wide-open generosity.

Teddy Blue, who knew her in Miles City's hey-day, said in an interview: "I've been on the plains for fifty-eight years, and I've never heard of an old-timer that knew her, but what spoke well of her."[15]

After Calamity Jane's confinement in the Bozeman poor house, the *Anaconda Standard* takes the same tone, with added editorial pomposity. "Like the buffalo and the distinctive characteristics of the plains and

[14] Dept. of History Collections, South Dakota, 1926, Vol. XIII, p. 35.
[15] Teddy Blue, "When I First Met Calamity Jane," 1928-1929, in a collection of stories compiled by I. D. O'Donnell on file at Billings, Montana Public Library.

mountains, she is a pathetic reminder of the vanishing glory of the old pioneer days and the free and easy life of the border."[16]

Estelline Bennett sensed the same feeling in a group which assembled to meet Calamity when she returned to Deadwood in 1895:

> But even before I had time to be disappointed, I sensed something about her that had assembled this group of the best pioneers to welcome her back to Deadwood. It was the most representative that the town could have assembled. Many among them were pioneers of '76, who in some way or other had known Calamity Jane in those early days. A few of them had come in a year or two later always regretting that their youth or some other trivial but insurmountable obstacle had held them back from the first dynamic rush into a life that never could be repeated . . .[17]

Later Miss Bennett says, "More than anyone else who lived into the twentieth century, Calamity Jane was symbolic of old Deadwood. Her virtues were of the endearing sort. Her vices were the wide-open sins of a wide-open country—the sort that never carried a hurt."[18]

Just after Calamity's death, the *Avant Courier* of Bozeman, Montana, where she had been in the poorhouse, quotes Buffalo Bill to the same effect. It has long been suspected that some things this renowned character wrote were more to enhance his own prestige than to record fact. An excerpt, however, will illustrate the tone:

> Only the old days could have produced her. She belongs to a time and a class that are fast disappearing . . . Calamity had nearly all the rough virtues

---

[16] *Anaconda Standard* (Butte, Montana), February 23, 1901.
[17] Estelline Bennett, pp. 221-222.
[18] *Ibid.*, p. 225.

of the old West as well as many of the vices . . .
She was one of the frontier types and she has all
the merits and most of their faults. There is no
frontier any more and never will be again, and that
is why we like to look back, and why the few that
remain of the old-timers we marched with and fought
with have a warm place in our affection, whatever
or wherever they may be.[19]

A far-fetched but interesting variant of this attitude
toward Calamity as "one of us" appeared in the *Fergus
County Argus* of Livingston, Montana, October 2, 1901,
when Calamity's fortune had reached a very low level:
"Calamity may not be possessed of all the feminine
graces but she is a better citizen than Emma Goldman
any day in the week."

REJECTION OF SOCIETY, PREFERENCE FOR THE FRONTIER:

There are frequent comments to urge that Calamity
Jane could act the lady when she wished or that she
rejected social luxuries for the open honest life of the
frontier:

Mokler in his *History of Natrona County* reports that
"some people say that Calamity had a wealth of knowledge and was familiar with the best of the social graces,
and was as much at home in a fine parlor as she was on
the range."[20] This author expresses grave doubts about
this opinion, but records its presence.

Brown and Willard discovered the same attitude toward her upon return from an exhibition in the East:

Once a kind-hearted woman of wealth sought to
lure her out of the slough and took her back to
Buffalo, but the lure of the hills was too strong and
Jane soon bade farewell to the stiff and conventional

---

[19] *Avant Courier* (Bozeman, Montana), August 7, 1903.
[20] Alfred James Mokler, *History of Natrona County, Wyoming, 1888-1922*, p. 434.

life of the East, and hastened back to the big hearted westerners.[21]

The same reaction was recorded by Connelley in his report of a visit she made to her old home in Missouri:

> She asked for leave to revisit her old home in Missouri. It was granted but the visit was a great disappointment to Jane. Calamity and the women of the stagnant little Missouri town had nothing in common. They regarded her as a curiosity, and were repelled by her uncouth and masculine ways.[22]

There is little reason to take much stock in this tale. It is not mentioned by any other writer, nor is it possible to imagine from whom Calamity asked leave. Its significance, like that of many other quotations in this chapter, is merely to show the characteristics out of which the frontiersman fabricated a heroine.

Several writers mention a marriage of Calamity Jane to a man named White in 1866[23] White was supposed to have become wealthy and taken Calamity to Denver where she was rigged out in fine clothes, free to enjoy the luxuries of civilization. It is always contended that she soon tired of this, threw the husband over and came back to "little old Deadwood."

Percy Russell, an old-timer who knew Calamity describes her marriage to White as follows:

> White sold out his property and became quite wealthy. He decided to quit the wilderness. He dressed his wife in the finest clothing to be had and departed to Denver. A few days of the fancy apparel and classy hotels was sufficient for the wild, untamed spirit of Martha Jane, and she made her escape.[24]

---

[21] Jessie Brown and A. M. Willard, p. 417.

[22] William Elsey Connelley, *Wild Bill and His Era*, p. 189.

[23] Estelline Bennett, p. 240; Jessie Brown and A. M. Willard, p. 413; Robert J. Casey, *The Black Hills and Their Incredible Characters*, p. 177.

[24] Percy Russell, *"Calamity Jane as Remembered by Percy Russell,"* an unpublished story in possession of Mr. Russell's estate.

Frackelton presents a similar evidence of this attitude. A man who knew Calamity told this dentist-author:

> That's Calamity! When she wants to be a lady she's as good as any of them. But let her go into a saloon, or a gambling joint, and she'll outswear any man in the place.[25]

Brown and Willard record the same view:

> She could swear like a trooper, drink like a sailor, and rough it with the roughest. Yet when sober, she could do the part of a real lady, and at all times was very fond of children, in whose presence she was watchful of her conduct.[26]

George Hoshier, an old-timer of Deadwood, did not go so far as to insist upon Jane's ladylike behavior, but he reflected the same feeling about her preference for the Black Hills: "But she'd no sooner get settled somewhere than she'd hear the wind in the pine trees, and see the lights in the gay old streets of little old Deadwood, and remember the boys and all, and she'd come back."[27]

THE-PITY-OF-IT COMMENTS:

Many of the writers about Calamity Jane take the attitude that the woman was the victim of circumstances or of an unfortunate childhood. A smattering of examples will illustrate this viewpoint.

An article published in the *Literary Digest* in 1925, states:

> While brave and kind, her moral side left much that was to be desired. If Calamity Jane was to a certain extent a social outcast, it was not entirely her fault. As one of the old Western ballads so admirably states the philosophy of the day:

---

[25] Will Frackelton, p. 124.
[26] Jessie Brown and A. M. Willard, p. 417.
[27] *Great Falls* (Montana) *Leader,* July 16, 1906.

The trail to the great mystic region
Is narrow and dim so they say.
While the one that leads to perdition
Is posted and blazed all the way,
Whose fault is it then that so many,
Go astray on this wild range, they fail
Who might have been rich and had plenty
Had they known of that dim narrow trail?[28]

Mokler, in his *History of Natrona County*, describes Calamity as a poor, neglected child who had no way of knowing right from wrong, who was lured to the effete East where she learned sinful ways.[29]

Captain Jack Crawford reflected something of this same point of view:

Calamity Jane was a good-hearted woman, under different environments would have made a good wife and mother . . . She grew up in a wild unnatural manner which we wonder did not quench out every spark of womanhood in her, and it is to her credit that she did retain a kind and generous heart even while following in the footsteps of her dissolute father and careless mother.[30]

LACK OF PRETENSE AND HYPOCRISY:

Calamity seems to have had, or at least has been credited with having another characteristic considered important and praiseworthy in frontier society. This was her lack of hypocrisy or pretense to virtues she did not possess, and her refusal to try to ingratiate herself with elements of law or respectability. Estelline Bennett recounts a story which illustrates this characteristic. A Deadwood lady, Mrs. Joe King, when asked for money by Calamity Jane, offered to buy her all the food she wanted, but refused to give her a cent to buy a drink.

[28] "Calamity Jane as a Lady Robinhood," *Literary Digest*, November 14, 1925 p. 47.
[29] Alfred James Mokler, p. 431.
[30] *Rapid City Journal* cited footnote eight.

Calamity blithely said she did not want food but a drink, and went good-naturedly on her way without stooping to pretend.[31]

Lewis Crawford mentions this characteristic. "While she lived a life of shame, yet she was as good as her associates. She never posed; her personality was her own.[32]

At a period when her fortunes had sunk very low, the *St. Paul Dispatch* said of this woman: "Jane has one recommendation, and that counts for considerable. She is perfectly willing to be what she seems to be and seem what she is."[33] To the frontiersman who looked upon the snobbery of the visiting English and the settled Easterner with disgust, this characteristic may well have counted for much, enough, along with the many good deeds she was credited with, to outweigh her flagrant misdeeds, if they needed outweighing in his mind.

These expressions of admiration from her friends indicate that she had certain good qualities like generosity, kindness and unselfishness. She loved the wild life of the frontier and disdained the cultured life of the east. These qualities were evident only in the minor events of her life. They gave way steadily to the dominant forces of drunkenness, whoring and violence. It is for the reader to judge whether the mild qualities should outweigh the more dominant ones.

---

[31] Estelline Bennett, p. 224-225.
[32] Lewis Crawford, *Rekindling Camp Fires,* p. 273.
[33] *St. Paul* (Minnesota) *Dispatch,* July 13, 1901.

LIFE AND ADVENTURES OF
CALAMITY JANE

By Herself

My maiden name was Marthy Cannary, was born in Princeton, Missourri, May 1st, 1852. Father and mother natives of Ohio. Had two brothers and three sisters, I being the oldest of the children. As a child I always had a fondness for adventure and out-door exercise and especial fondness for horses which I began to ride at an early age and continued to do so until I became an expert rider being able to ride the most vicious and stubborn of horses, in fact the greater portion of my life in early times was spent in this manner.

In 1865 we emigrated from our homes in Missourri by the overland route to Virginia City, Montana, taking five months to make the journey. While on the way the greater portion of my time was spent in hunting along with the men and hunters of the party, in fact I was at all times with the men when there was excitement and adventures to be had. By the time we reached Virginia City I was considered a remarkable good shot and a fearless rider for a girl of my age. I remember many occurrences on the journey from Missourri to Montana. Many times in crossing the mountains the conditions of the trail were so bad that we frequently had to lower the wagons over ledges by hand with ropes for they were so rough and rugged that horses were of no use. We also had many exciting times fording streams for many of the streams in our way were noted for quicksands and boggy places, where, unless we were very careful, we would have lost horses and all. Then we had many dangers to encounter in the way of streams swelling on account of heavy rains. On occasions of that kind the men would usually select the best places to cross the streams, myself on more than one occasion have mounted my pony and swam across the stream several times merely to amuse myself and have had many narrow escapes from having both myself and pony washed away to certain death, but as the pioneers of those days had plenty of courage we overcame all obstacles and reached Virginia City in safety.

Mother died at Black Foot, Montana, 1866, where we buried her. I left Montana in Spring of 1866, for Utah, arriving at Salt Lake city during the summer. Remained in Utah until 1867, where my father died, then went to Fort Bridger, Wyoming Territory, where we arrived May 1, 1868. Remained around Fort Bridger during 1868, then went to Piedmont, Wyoming, with U. P. Railway. Joined General Custer as a scout at Fort Russell, Wyoming, in 1870, and started for Arizona for the Indian Campaign. Up to this time I had always worn the costume of my sex. When I joined Custer I donned the uniform of a soldier. It was a bit awkward at first but I soon got to be perfectly at home in men's clothes.

Was in Arizona up to the winter of 1871 and during that time I had a great many adventures with the Indians, for as a scout I had a great many dangerous missions to perform and while I was in many close places always succeeded in getting away safely for by this time I was considered the most reckless and daring rider and one of the best shots in the western country.

After that campaign I returned to Fort Sanders, Wyoming, remained there until spring of 1872, when we were ordered out to the Muscle Shell or Nursey Pursey Indian outbreak. In that war Generals Custer, Miles, Terry and Crook were all engaged. This campaign lasted until fall of 1873.

It was during this campaign that I was christened Calamity Jane. It was on Goose Creek, Wyoming, where the town of Sheridan is now located. Capt. Egan was in command of the Post. We were ordered out to quell an uprising of the Indians, and were out for several days, had numerous skirmishes during which six of the soldiers were killed and several severely wounded. When on returning to the Post we were ambushed about a mile and a half from our destination. When fired upon Capt. Egan was shot. I was riding in advance and on hearing the firing turned in my saddle and saw the Captain reeling in his saddle as though about to fall. I turned my horse and galloped back with all haste to his side and got there in time to catch him as he was falling. I lifted him onto my horse in front of me and succeeded in getting him safely to the Fort. Capt. Egan on recovering, laughingly said: "I name you Calamity Jane, the heroine of the plains." I have borne that name up to the present time. We were afterwards ordered to Fort Custer, where Custer city now stands, where we arrived in the spring of 1874; remained around Fort Custer all summer and were ordered to Fort Russell in the fall of 1874, where we remained until spring of 1875; was then ordered to the Black Hills to protect miners, as that country was controlled by the Sioux Indians and the government had to send the soldiers to protect the lives of the miners and settlers in that section. Remained there until fall of 1875 and wintered at Fort Laramie. In spring of 1876, we were ordered north with General Crook to join Gen'ls Miles, Terry and Custer at Big Horn river. During this march I swam the Platte river at Fort Fetterman as I was the bearer of important dispatches. I had a ninety mile ride to make, being wet and cold, I contracted a severe illness and was sent back in Gen. Crook's ambulance to Fort Fetterman where I laid in the hospital for fourteen days. When able to ride I started for Fort Laramie where I met Wm. Hickok, better known as Wild Bill, and we started for Deadwood, where we arrived about June.

During the month of June I acted as a pony express rider carrying the U. S. mail between Deadwood and Custer, a distance of fifty miles, over one of the roughest trails in the Black Hills country. As many of the riders before me had been held up and robbed of their packages, mail and money that they carried, for that was the only means of getting mail and money between

these points. It was considered the most dangerous
route in the Hills, but as my reputation as a rider and
quick shot was well known, I was molested very little,
for the toll gatherers looked on me as being a good
fellow, and they knew that I never missed my mark.
I made the round trip every two days which was considered pretty good riding in that country. Remained
around Deadwood all that summer visiting all the camps
within an area of one hundred miles. My friend, Wild
Bill, remained in Deadwood during the summer with
the exception of occasional visits to the camps. On the
2nd of August, while setting at a gambling table in the
Bell Union saloon, in Deadwood, he was shot in the
back of the head by the notorious Jack McCall, a desperado. I was in Deadwood at the time and on hearing
of the killing made my way at once to the scene of
the shooting and found that my friend had been killed
by McCall. I at once started to look for the assassian
and found him at Shurdy's butcher shop and grabbed a
meat cleaver and made him throw up his hands; through
the excitement on hearing of Bill's death, having left
my weapons on the post of my bed. He was then taken
to a log cabin and locked up, well secured as every one
thought, but he got away and was afterwards caught at
Fagan's ranch on Horse Creek, on the old Cheyenne
road and was then taken to Yankton, Dak., where he
was tried, sentenced and hung.

I remained around Deadwood locating claims, going
from camp to camp until the spring of 1877, where one
morning, I saddled my horse and rode towards Crook
city. I had gone about twelve miles from Deadwood, at
the mouth of Whitewood creek, when I met the overland mail running from Cheyenne to Deadwood. The
horses on a run, about two hundred yards from the station; upon looking closely I saw they were pursued by
Indians. The horses ran to the barn as was their custom. As the horses stopped I rode along side of the
coach and found the driver John Slaughter, lying face
downwards in the boot of the stage, he having been

shot by the Indians. When the stage got to the station the Indians hid in the bushes. I immediately removed all baggage from the coach except the mail. I then took the driver's seat and with all haste drove to Deadwood, carrying the six passengers and the dead driver.

I left Deadwood in the fall of 1877, and went to Bear Butte Creek with the 7th Cavalry. During the fall and winter we built Fort Meade and the town of Sturgis. In 1878 I left the command and went to Rapid city and put in the year prospecting.

In 1879, I went to Fort Pierre and drove trains from Rapid city to Fort Pierre for Frank Witcher then drove teams from Fort Pierre to Sturgis for Fred. Evans. This teaming was done with oxen as they were better fitted for the work than horses, owing to the rough nature of the country.

In 1881 I went to Wyoming and returned in 1882 to Miles City and took up a ranch on the Yellow Stone, raising stock and cattle, also kept a way side inn, where the weary traveler could be accommodated with food, drink, or trouble if he looked for it. Left the ranch in 1883, went to California, going through the States and territories, reached Ogden the latter part of 1883, and San Francisco in 1884. Left San Francisco in the summer of 1884 for Texas, stopping at Fort Yuma, Arizona, the hottest spot in the United States. Stopping at all points of interest until I reached El Paso in the fall. While in El Paso, I met Mr. Clinton Burk, a native of Texas, who I married in August 1885. As I thought I had travelled through life long enough alone and thought it was about time to take a partner for the rest of my days. We remained in Texas leading a quiet home life until 1889. On October 28th, 1887, I became the mother of a girl baby, the very image of its father, at least that is what he said, but who has the temper of its mother.

When we left Texas we went to Boulder, Colo., where we kept a hotel until 1893, after which we travelled through Wyoming, Montana, Idaho, Washington, Oregon, then back to Montana, then to Dakota, arriving in Deadwood October 9th, 1895, after an absence of seventeen years.

My arrival in Deadwood after an absence so many years created quite an excitement among my many friends of the past, to such an extent that a vast number of the citizens who had come to Deadwood during my absence who had heard so much of Calamity Jane and her many adventures in former years were anxious to see me. Among the many whom I met were several gentlemen from eastern cities, who advised me to allow myself to be placed before the public in such a manner as to give the people of the eastern cities an opportunity of seeing the Woman Scout who was made so famous through her daring career in the West and the Black Hill countries.

An agent of Kohl & Middleton, the celebrated Museum men came to Deadwood, through the solicitation of the gentleman whom I met there and arrangements were made to place me before the public in this manner. My first engagement began at the Palace Museum, Minneapolis, January 20th, 1896, under Kohl and Middleton's management.

Hoping that this little history of my life may interest all readers. I remain as in the older days,

Yours,

Mrs. M. Burk, (Dorsett.)
Better Known As Calamity Jane
(1896)

BIBLIOGRAPHY

Sources

(A) NEWSPAPERS

Every contemporary newspaper account found by the writer in which there is any mention of Calamity Jane is listed whether or not it is used in this study. Included are notices of Calamitys other than Martha Cannary. These newspapers were located after many weeks' search in the towns listed below. The *Union List of Newspapers* is by no means complete. Small libraries and newspaper publishing offices sometimes have complete files of local papers which are not listed in that volume. Those are starred before the name of the paper. Contemporary newspaper notices of Calamity Jane are perhaps the most accurate source of information. They usually are short but give enough information to establish her whereabouts and describe her uproarious activities.

Anaconda Standard (Anaconda, Montana), February 23, 1901. Montana Historical Society.

Avant Courier (Bozeman, Montana), August 7, 1903. Montana Historical Society.

Billings (Montana) *Gazette,* November 25, December 16, 1902. Montana Historical Society.

Black Hills Daily Pioneer (Deadwood, South Dakota), May 29, 1879. Minnesota Historical Society.

*Black Hills Daily Times (Deadwood, South Dakota), September 21 and 22, 1877; September 24, 1878; October 5 and 6, November 14, 16, and 17, December 12, 1895; January 9 and 16, 1896. Deadwood, South Dakota Public Library, not in Union List.

*Black Hills Press (Sturgis, South Dakota), January 10, 1896. In the office of the only newspaper published in Sturgis, South Dakota, not in Union List.

Black Hills Weekly Champion (Central City, South Dakota), December 2, 1877. Minnesota Historical Society.

*Black Hills Weekly Times (Deadwood, South Dakota), November 9, 1895. Deadwood, South Dakota Public Library, not in Union List.

Carbon County Journal (Rawlins, Wyoming), December 20, 1884; July 25, 1885; September 18, October 30, November 6, 1886; October 12, 1895. Rawlins, Wyoming Public Library.

Casper (Wyoming) *Weekly Mail,* October 11, 1889. Casper, Wyoming Public Library.

Cheyenne (Wyoming) *Daily Leader,* June 20, July 30, November 23, 1876; January 26, July 7, 1877; June 6, December 10, 1879; May 16, 1883; November 3, 1885; June 21, 1887. Wyoming Historical Society.

Cheyenne (Wyoming) *Daily Sun,* July 7, 1877. Wyoming Historical Society.

Daily Independent (Helena), September 18, 1896; April 3, 1901. Montana Historical Society.

Daily Press and Dakotian (Yankton, South Dakota), August 8, 1877. South Dakota Historical Society.

Daily Register-Call (Central City, Colorado), August 27, 1878. Colorado Historical Society.

Democratic Leader (Cheyenne, Wyoming), November 25, 1884; March 21, 1885; March 12, 1887. Wyoming Historical Society.

Denver (Colorado) *Daily Times,* August 17, 22 and 26, 1878. Colorado Historical Society.

Fergus County Argus (Lewistown, Montana), October 2, 1901. Montana Historical Society.

Great Falls (Montana) *Leader,* July 16, 1906. Montana Historical Society.

Helena (Montana) *Evening Herald,* July 16, 1901. Montana Historical Society.

Laramie (Wyoming) *Boomerang,* February 28, 1887, August 30, September 26, 1889. University of Wyoming Library.

Livingston (Montana) *Enterprise,* June 12, 1886; September 17, 1887. Montana Historical Society.

Livingston (Montana) *Post,* April 24, June 5, 1902; August 6, 1903. Montana Historical Society.

Minneapolis (Minnesota) *Journal,* January 20, 1896. Minnesota Historical Society.

Montana Post (Virginia City), December 31, 1864. Montana Historical Society.

Montana Weekly Record (Helena), June 3, 1902. Montana Historical Society.

New North-West (Deer Lodge, Montana), February 10, 1882. Montana Historical Society.

*Pioneer-Times (Deadwood, South Dakota), October 5, 1895, June 6, 1896; June 25, August 2, 5 and 8, 1903; June 20, 1951 citing the *Pioneer* (Deadwood, South Dakota), July 13, 1876. Deadwood, South Dakota Public Library, not in Union List.

River Press (Fort Benton, Montana), May 31, 1882. Montana Historical Society.

Rocky Mountain News (Denver Colorado), June 10, 1877; January 11, August 23, 1878. Colorado Historical Society.

Semi-Weekly Miner (Butte, Montana), December 6, 1882. Montana Historical Society.

*Sidney (Nebraska) *Telegraph,* August 4, 1877. Sidney, Nebraska Public Library, not in Union List.

St. Paul (Minnesota) *Dispatch,* July 13, 1901. Minnesota Historical Society.

Weekly Signal (Fort Pierre, Dakota), July 21, 1880. South Dakota Historical Society.

Yellowstone Journal (Miles City, Montana), February 11, May 31, June 3, July 1, 8 and 15, August 5 and 12, September 2, November 11 and 25, December 6 and 16, 1882; March 3, 1883; August 8, 1885. Montana Historical Society.

(B) GOVERNMENT DOCUMENTS

U. S. Geographical and Geological Survey of the Rocky Mountain Region, *Report on the Geology and Resources of the Black Hills of Dakota, with Atlas,* by Henry Newton and Walter P. Jennez. (Washington, Government Printing Office, 1880.)

(C) DIARIES

Burk, Martha, *Life and Adventures of Calamity Jane by Herself,* place of publication unknown, publisher unknown, 1896.

"David Holmes Diary" *Collections of the State Historical Society,* Vol. V., O. G. Libby, Editor, (Grand Forks, North Dakota: 1923). One sentence pertaining to Calamity Jane.

(D) UNPUBLISHED MATERIAL

Unpublished diary of I. N. Bard is in the Agnes Wright Spring Collection, Western History Department, Denver Public Library, Denver, Colorado. One sentence pertaining to Calamity Jane.

Percy Russell, *Calamity Jane as Remembered by Percy Russell,* in possession of Mr. Russell's estate in Deadwood, South Dakota.

E. C. Abbott (Teddy Blue) "When I First Met Calamity Jane," in a collection of stories compiled by I. D. O'Donnell on file at Billings, Montana Public Library.

Memoirs of Richard B. Hughes, in possession of Richard B. Hughes, Jr., of Rapid City, South Dakota.

PERSONAL INTERVIEWS

Mr. William Berry (Missoula, Montana)

Mr. George Simon (Livingston, Montana)

Mr. Fred Sumner (Livingston, Montana)

Mr. Walter C. Nye (Billings, Montana)

Mr. Edward L. Senn (Deadwood, South Dakota)

Mr. D. M. McGahey (Deadwood, South Dakota)

Mr. Charles Fales (Fort Pierre, South Dakota)

Mr. Al Hildebrandt (Pierre, South Dakota)

Mrs. M. J. Schubert (Pierre, South Dakota)

Mrs. Mary Robinson (Spearfish, South Dakota)

Mr. John Sohn (Deadwood, South Dakota)

Mr. Percy Russell (Deadwood, South Dakota)

Two nuns at St. Martin's Convent (Sturgis, South Dakota)

SECONDARY WORKS

(A) BOOKS

The books below contain anywhere from a few sentences to a few pages about Calamity Jane. Usually the story of her life is reviewed only as general background material for some important frontier movement in which she figured as one of the numerous interesting but unimportant characters. Only five writers find her important enough to use her as the subject of an entire book. Those writers are Dee, Hueston, Mumey, Plunkett and Spencer. The narratives of Hueston, Spencer and von Schmidt-Paul may be considered pure fiction. The most objective account of Calamity is the one by McClintock. There are only five pages in his book devoted to that woman but they contain valuable information. McClintock's word is always as honest and accurate as can be given by someone writing years after an event. He differentiates between what he saw from what he heard. Second hand information he evaluates according to the person who told it and the circumstances surrounding it. Aikman's book has been widely quoted but is highly fictionalized. However, after careful reading, his colored account shows historical research. Mumey has assembled almost all the facts of Calamity Jane to date in his book. It includes a facsimile of the *Autobiography*, nearly every picture reproduced in other books, the complete diary claimed by Mrs. Jane Hickok McCormick to be Calamity Jane's and a good collection of newspaper items of Calamity quoted in full. Mumey does little in the way of organizing his material or drawing conclusions.

Abbott, E. C. and Smith, Helena Huntington, *We Pointed Them North*, (New York: Farrar & Rinehart, Inc., 1939).

Aikman, Duncan, *Calamity Jane and the Lady Wildcats*, (New York: Blue Ribbon Books, Inc., 1927).

Allen, William A., *Adventures with Indians and Game* (Chicago: A. W. Bowen & Co., 1903).

Bennett, Estelline, *Old Deadwood Days*, (New York: Charles Scribner's Sons, 1935).

"John Edmund, Boland River Man—His Recollections as Told by Bert Hall," South Dakota State Historical Collections, (Pierre: State Publishing Co., 1947) Vol. XXIII.

Bourke, John Gregory, *On the Border with Crook*, (New York: C. Scribner's Sons, 1891).

Briggs, Harold E., *Frontiers of the Northwest*, (New York: D. Appleton-Century Co., 1940).

Brininstool, Earl A., *Fighting Red Cloud's Warriors*, (Columbus, Ohio: The Hunter-Trapper-Trader Co., 1926). (Juvenile book.)

Brown, Jessie and Willard, A. M., *The Black Hills Trails*, edited by John T. Milek, (Rapid City, S. D.: Rapid City Journal Co., 1924).

Brown, Thomas Henderson, *Romance of Everyday Life*, (Mitchell, South Dakota: Educator Supply Co., 1923).

Casey, Robert J., *The Black Hills and Their Magnificent Characters*, (Indianapolis & New York: Bobbs-Merrill Co., Inc., 1949).

Connelley, William Elsey, *Wild Bill & His Era*, (New York: The Press of the Pioneers, 1933).

Coursey, O. W. *Beautiful Black Hills,* (Mitchell, South Dakota: Educator Supply Co., 1926).

Crawford, Lewis F., *Rekindling Camp Fires,* (Bismarck, North Dakota: Capital Book Co., 1926).

Cunningham, Eugene, *Triggernometry,* (New York: The Press of the Pioneers, Inc., 1934).

Dee, D., *Low Down on Calamity Jane,* (Rapid City, South Dakota: no publisher mentioned—1932).

Deland, Charles E., *The Sioux Wars,* South Dakota State Historical Collections, (Pierre: Hipple Printing Co., 1930) Vol. XV.

Eisele, Wilbert Edwin, *The Real Wild Bill Hickok,* (Denver: W. H. Andre, 1931).

Frackelton, Dr. Will, *Sagebrush Dentist,* edited by Herman G. Seely, (Chicago: A. C. McClurg & Co., 1941).

Freeman, Lewis R., *Down the Yellowstone,* (New York: Dodd, Mead & Co., 1922).

Henry, Ralph C. (Eric Thane, pseudo) *High Border Country,* (New York: Duell, Sloan & Pearce, 1942).

Holbrook, Stewart H., *Little Annie Oakley and Other Rugged People,* (New York: The MacMillan Co., 1948).

Holmes, Burton, *Travelogues,* (Chicago & New York: The Travelogue Bureau, 1914) Vol. 12.

Hueston, Ethel, *Calamity Jane of Deadwood Gulch,* (Indianapolis & New York: Bobbs-Merrill Co., 1937).

Kate C. McBeth, *The Nez Perces Since Lewis and Clark,* (New York: Fleming H. Revell Co., 1908).

McClintock, John S., *Pioneer Days in the Black Hills,* edited by Edward L. Senn, (Deadwood, South Dakota: John S. McClintock, 1939).

McGillycuddy, Julia B., *McGillycuddy Agent* (Stanford University California: Stanford University Press, 1941).

McPherren, Ida., *Imprints on Pioneer Trails,* (Boston: Christopher Publishing House, 1950).

Maguire, Horatio N., *The Coming Empire,* (Sioux City, Iowa: Watkins & Smead, 1878).

Mills, Anson, (Brig. Gen. U.S.A.) *My Story,* edited by C. H. Claudy, (Washington, D. C.: Press of Byron S Adams, 1918)

Milner, Joe E. and Forrest, Earle R., *California Joe,* (Caldwell, Idaho: The Caxton Printers, Ltd., 1935).

Mokler, Alfred James, *History of Natrona County, Wyoming,* 1888-1922, (Chicago: R. R. Donnelley & Sons Co., The Lakeside Press, 1923).

Mumey, Nolie, *Calamity Jane* 1852-1903, (Denver: The Range Press, 1950).

Nelson, Bruce O., *Land of the Dacotahs,* (Minneapolis: University of Minnesota Press, 1946).

Otero, Miguel Antonio, *My Life on the Frontier,* (New York: The Press of the Pioneers Inc., 1935).

Plunkett, Ierne Arthur Lifford, *Calamity Jane* (Clarion Series) (Toronto, Canada: 1935, Oxford University Press).

Quiett, Glenn Chesney, *Pay Dirt,* (New York: D. Appleton-Century Co., 1936).

Rogers, Agnes, *Women Are Here to Stay,* (New York: Harper & Bros. Publishers, 1949).

Sabin, Edwin Legrand, *Wild Men of the Wild West,* (New York: Thomas Y. Cromwell Co., 1929).

Schmitt, Martin F. and Brown, Dee, *Fighting Indians of the West,* (New York: Charles Scribner's Sons, 1948).

Senn, Edward L., *"Deadwood Dick and Calamity Jane,"* (Deadwood, South Dakota, Edward L. Senn, 1939).

Spencer, Mrs. George, *Calamity Jane; A Story of the Black Hills,* (no city, no publisher, 1887).

Sutley, Zack T., *The Last Frontier,* (New York: Macmillan Co., 1930).

Van de Water, Frederic F., *Glory Hunter,* (Indianapolis: The Bobbs-Merrill Co., 1934).

von Schmidt-Paul, Edgar, *We Indians, The Passing of a Great Race,* (New York: E. P. Dutton & Co. Inc., 1931).

Westerners Brand Book, 1945-46, edited by Manuel Hahn (Chicago: The Brand Book, 1947).

Westerners Brand Book, 1944, edited by members of Westerners (Chicago: The Brand Book, 1946).

Whittaker, Frederick, *The Life of General George A. Custer* (New York: Sheldon & Co., 1876).

Wilstach, Frank J., *Wild Bill Hickok,* (Garden City N. Y.: Doubleday, Page & Co., 1926).

Young, Harry (Sam), *Hard Knocks,* (Chicago: Laird & Lee, Inc., 1915).

(B) PERIODICALS

"Calamity Jane as a Lady Robinhood," *Literary Digest,* XXCVII (November 14, 1925).

"Jane Canary, 1852-1903," *Pony Express,* (February, 1946).

Asbury, Herbert, "Six Sinful Sirens," *Hearst's International Cosmopolitan,* CI (December, 1936).

Brininstool, E. A., "Calamity Jane, The Most Unique, Picturesque and Romantic Figure in Black Hills History," *Hunter, Trader, Trapper,* (June and July 1925).

Freeman, Lewis R., "Calamity Jane and Yankee Jim," *Sunset Magazine,* XLIX (July, 1922).

Hilton, Francis W., "Calamity Jane," *Frontier,* (September, 1925).

Holbrook, Stewart H., "Calamity Jane," *American Mercury,* LXIV (February, 1947).

Holbrook, Stewart H., "Wild Bill Hickok There Was a Man," *Esquire,* (May, 1950).

Ledyard, Edgar M., "American Forts," *Utah Historical Quarterly* I, (October, 1928).

Nelson, Bruce O., "The Myth of Calamity Jane," *Adventure*, (December, 1943).

Phillips, Paul C., "The Life and Adventures of Calamity Jane," *Frontier and Midland*, XVI (Summer, 1936).

Reckless Ralph, "Calamity Jane, Queen of the Plains," *Street and Smith's New York Weekly*, XXXVII (January 16-March 13, 1882).

Smith, Arthur D. Howden, "Women America Remembers, VIII, Calamity Jane," *Hearst's International Cosmopolitan*(?), date missing but pages are 26-27, 143. This article is on file in the Montana folder at Montana State University.

Wagner, Glendolin Damon, "Calamity Jane," *Montana Oil and Mining Journal*, (January, 1936).

PICTURE NOTES

No. 1. This is one picture of Calamity Jane which has been challenged by some historians who believe that it really pictures Mattie Young, a notorious woman of Denver who before her death in a buggy accident in 1878 was known as Calamity Jane. She was as dissolute in her habits as the real Calamity Jane, but she was much more feminine in appearance and never dressed in men's clothing. Furthermore, she confined her activities to Denver and vicinity. The handwriting at the bottom of the picture is known to be that of C. S. (Mountain Charlie) Stobie, a frontier character who delighted in having his picture taken with notables of his day. Mrs. Agnes Wright Spring, Historian of the State Historical Society of Colorado, who used the picture in her book, "Cheyenne and Black Hills Stage Routes," says that it is believed certain that Mountain Charlie knew the real Calamity Jane and that he would make an accurate identification. It is certainly true, too, that Captain Jack Crawford knew the Black Hills Calamity Jane well. Attempts to accurately date this interesting picture have been unsuccessful. The firm of Willis & Clyde which did the mounting were in business in Denver as early as 1901. However, the Denver Public Library, which owns the original, believes the picture was taken much earlier than the mounting would indicate.

* * *

Note 2. Teddy Blue (E. C.) Abbott, who became a son-in-law of Granville Stuart, was a cowboy in the classic wild and woolly pattern and would never turn down a drink in circumstances such as this picture depicts. In his book, "We Pointed Them North," Blue said he first met Calamity Jane in the Black Hills in 1878. In his words: "She was dressed in purple velvet, with diamonds on her and everything. As I recall it, she was some sort of a madam at that time, running a great big gambling hall in Deadwood." He states he met her again in Miles City in the Fall of 1883 and "bought her a few drinks." He light-heartedly borrowed 50c from her when they met on the Miles City-Deadwood stage line in the Winter of 1883 and promised to pay her back the money some day. His book says that he did not see her again for 24 years, and that was at Gilt Edge in 1907. Since Calamity Jane died in 1903, the old cowboy is incorrect in his dates, but this picture indicates that they did indeed meet in Gilt Edge and at one time at least lifted a glass together. Blue always spoke highly of Calamity Jane's warm-heartedness.

* * *

Note 3. Charles Haas of Deadwood has related in his own words the circumstances under which he took this picture of the sick and aging Calamity Jane in Whitewood, S. D., in the summer of 1903, not long before her death. She was drifting back to Deadwood after a trip to Montana and Wyoming, and even though her health was deteriorating rapidly, she

139

continued to drink heavily. Haas' story is quoted below as it originally appeared in "Calamity Jane of the Western Trails" by J. Leonard Jennewein. Jennewein, who is on the faculty of South Dakota Wesleyan University at Mitchell, S. D., has done much research into the life of Calamity Jane before and since his publication appeared in 1953 and has been of great assistance to the publishers of this book. Haas' story follows:

"Well, the way I came by this picture was like this. I was in Whitewood one day, and I had my camera, cameras weren't common in those days; mine had glass plates and I was going over to where some of my relatives lived and take some pictures of their young folks when I met Calamity on the street. 'Hello,' she says. 'Where are you going?' 'I'm going to take some pictures of the family,' I said. 'Oh,' Calamity said. 'Would you take a picture of me?' And I said, 'Sure, I'll be only too glad to, Calamity.' So I hopped off this old board sidewalk and took the picture and Calamity says, 'Now, how about a couple of drinks?' And I said that was just fine so we went across the street into the saloon, that would be Jackson and Gustine's Saloon. Calamity was down there quite a lot and I called for drinks and was wishing her luck when I had a thought; this saloon had those tokens that you paid with, and I thought I'd like to keep the token that I paid for her drink with so I slipped over another quarter and he gave me a couple more tokens and I slid mine over to her. 'This is yours, Calamity,' then I took it away from her and gave her the other one. 'What are you up to?' Calamity said. 'I want the token I gave you as a keepsake,' I said. 'Oh, that's very nice,' said Calamity. And that's how I came by the picture and the token on my watch fob.

"And don't you know that there were just lots of people in that little old town who had kind words for Calamity. She was outstanding, that woman was; it was down in her heart and if she had a chance to do succor for somebody and to help them out of a tight place she was right there. Lots of us in Whitewood, and here in Deadwood, too, knew the better side of Calamity; but then, you know, she would go to these bawdy houses and dance halls and it was whoopee and soon she was drunk and then, well, things just sort of went haywire with old Calamity."

*   *   *

Note 4. Considerable research indicates that this particular pose of Calamity Jane at Wild Bill's grave shortly before her death was taken by John B. Mayo of Lead, S. Dak. or by a photographer from the Peterson Studio in Deadwood. Percy Russell, who died late in 1957, related to the author of this book that he remembered Calamity Jane going to Wild Bill's grave to have her picture taken, and it is possible that other pictures were taken which have not come to light. John Sohn, who operated a bootery shop in Deadwood, also recalled this occasion or one like it. He said Calamity came by his shop in a hack and when asked where she was going, she said she was on her way to Mt. Moriah Cemetery to have her picture taken. J. Leonard Jennewein of Mitchell, S. Dak., in researching for his book "Calamity Jane of the Western Trails," received much material from Mr. Mayo concerning this picture and another supposedly taken the same day in which he himself posed with Calamity Jane by the iron fence surrounding Wild Bill's grave. Some of this material may be whimsical, but it is interesting. Mayo and some companions had met Calamity Jane in Wyoming earlier in the summer of 1903 and Calamity told Mayo she would be returning to the Black Hills after July 4 and would be glad to pose for him at Wild Bill's grave in Deadwood. Mayo continues: "She came to Lead in the evening of about the 20th of July and told me where I could find her next day in Deadwood. I took a man along from Lead to carry the camera and tripod and after looking for her, Sidney Jacobs told us she was in a Chinese laundry back of the Mansion Hotel. I suggested hiring a hack to drive to the cemetery but she wanted to walk. The dress she wore that day was a bright red and a sunbonnet of the same color. As the bonnet covered her face I replaced it with a white hat my companion was wearing. While I was setting up the camera she said if I was too good to have a picture with her, I could go to the Hot Place. I then stood by the fence and my companion pressed the bulb. (This picture of Calamity and Mayo first appeared in the Rapid City, S. D. *Daily Journal* on September 28, 1952. It was said to have been hidden away for nearly a half century.) I put in another plate and took one of her standing alone by the iron fence. The picture was taken about 10 days before she died."

* * *

Note 5. The original of this picture of Calamity Jane is in possession of the author of this book. It was given to her by Mrs. Mary Robinson, widow of the undertaker, Charles Robinson, during an interview in July, 1949. Mrs. Robinson had the picture along with other relics of the past, and turned it over to Mrs. Sollid with the understanding that no commercial use ever made of it. This kind of sensational picture obviously is in demand by people who make tourist postcards and otherwise capitalize on the notoriety of Calamity Jane. The publishers of this book experienced some hesitation before including this gloomy picture in these pages, both because there was a question of taste and because there was a possibility of its reproduction by unauthorized persons. It is believed that it has enough historic interest to warrant publishing, and should serve to affix a finality to this appraisal of Calamity Jane. A copy of this picture has been placed in the files of the Historical Society of Montana, but any reproduction of it for any reason is prohibited without direct permission.

INDEX

Fort Laramie, Wyoming, 5-6, 8-9, 26, 29-30, 32, 35, 41-42, 127
Fort Laramie Treaty of 1868, 25
Fort Leavenworth, Kansas, 24
Fort Meade, South Dakota, 129
Fort Pierre, South Dakota, 69-70, 73, 129
Fort Pierre and Black Hills Transportation Co., 70
Fort Sanders, Wyoming, 34, 126-127
Fort Washakie, Lander, Wyoming, 51
Fort Yuma, Arizona, 129
Fowler, Helen, as accompanist at Calamity Jane's funeral, 108
Frackelton, Will, 52, 95, 115, 122
Frank, F. (Minnie Watson, another Calamity Jane), 21
Freeman, Lewis, 10-11
Funeral of Calamity Jane, 107-109

Gallagher, Major, 17
Gibbon, General John, 28, 31, 37
Gladdis, "Old Mother," 86
Goldman, Emma, 120
Good old days, attitudes toward Calamity Jane as a symbol of, 118-120
Goose Creek (Sheridan, Wyoming), 18, 35, 37-38, 126
Goose Creek incident, 18, 35, 37-38, 126
Granada, Colorado, 18
Great American Desert, 72
Gruard, Frank, 31

Hays City, Kansas, 17
Heart-of-gold vindication, of Calamity Jane,, 113-118
Heater, Gabriel, 44
Hebard, Grace, 6
Hendricks, A. R., 13
Hickok, William (Wild Bill), as supposed husband of Calamity Jane, 7, 39, 41-45, 93, 98-100, 105-106, 109-110, 116, 127-128
Holbrook, Stewart H., 27n, 61, 93
Hollywood films on Calamity Jane, xi, 93
Homestake Mining Company, 71

Hopkins, George S., pallbearer for Calamity Jane, 109
Horr, Montana, 79
Horse Creek, South Dakota, 99
Hoshier, George, 33, 61-62, 117, 122
Hot Springs, South Dakota, 89
Howard, General O. O., 37
Hughes, Richard B., 42, 43n

Iler, Walker, 101

Jackson, Ed, 91
Jackson, Sam, 103
James, Jesse, 33-34
Jenney, Walter P., 25-26
Jenney Expedition, 5-6, 8, 24-28
Joan of Arc, Calamity Jane characterized as, xivn, 114

Kansas Pacific Railroad, 17-18
"Kentucky Belle;" alias Mrs. Opie, alias Calamity Jane, 22
King, Frank, as husband of Calamity Jane, 22
King, Mrs. Joe, 123
King, Mrs. Martha, as supposed married name of Calamity Jane, 52-53
Kit Carson, Colorado, 18
Kitty, the Schemer, 39
Kohl & Middleton, museum managers, 75, 130

Lack of pretense and hypocrisy, of Calamity Jane, 123-124
Lady Robinhood, Calamity Jane characterized as, xiv
LaJunta, Colorado, 18
Lake and Northern Boundary Surveys, 25
Lander, Wyoming, 51-52
Laramie, Wyoming, 21-22, 38, 85-86
Laramie Boomerang, 38
Ledyard, Edgard M., 24n
Literary Digest, 122-123
Livingston, Montana, 22, 45, 47-50, 64, 79, 82, 86, 89, 95, 120

McCall, Jack, 98-100, 128
McClintock, John S., 12-13, 16, 42-43, 54, 73, 99

Both *The Plainsman* (1936), starring Jean Arthur and Gary Cooper (above), and *Calamity Jane* (1953), starring Doris Day, fueled the myth of a serious romance between Calamity Jane and Wild Bill Hickok, and glossed over the real Calamity's more undesirable traits. (Courtesy Paul Andrew Hutton)

CALAMITY JANE
CREATION OF A WESTERN LEGEND
An Afterword by Richard W. Etulain

Visualize on screen a young woman, pretty in form-fitting buckskins, lashing up teams of horses struggling to control a stagecoach careening down a dusty frontier incline. In the midst of this brief but eye-catching scenario, a complex figure begins to emerge. The attractive, vivacious female is also a rambunctious, adventuresome woman, involved in frontiersmen's work. Gradually, scene by scene, the leather-clad figure fades out, replaced by a romantic, feminine heroine coming into sharper focus, until the mannish protagonist entirely disappears.

Here, in the transformation of Doris Day in the musical Western *Calamity Jane* (1953), was a central dilemma facing legend-makers: how could a picaresque, often ribald and risqué Calamity Jane be transformed into an acceptable romantic heroine? Another contradiction seemed equally problematic. Since so little was known about Martha Jane Canary, should moviemakers, novelists, and other purveyors of popular culture begin in the middle of her life, *in medias res*, with such intriguing but unsubstantiated stories as her alleged romance with Wild Bill Hickok, her service with George Crook and George Custer, or her appearance in Buffalo Bill's Wild West?

Arriving about halfway between Calamity's death in 1903 and the present, Doris Day's Calamity illustrated both the romantic Wild West heroine invented during the previous half century and more, as well as the figure that gray, ambivalent Calamities of the post-1960s replaced. If the central character of *Calamity Jane* epitomized the frontier heroines of film and fiction of the pre-1950s era, she differed markedly from the darker, less vivacious Calamities that novelists such as Pete Dexter and Larry McMurtry created in the past generation. After the 1950s and 1960s, popularizers never returned to the naive tomboy Doris Day played in the 1950s. But even that earlier romantic image of Calamity did not take hold overnight. Although Calamity starred in dime novels when barely out of her teens, as something of a legend in her own time, the first extensive biography and important movie of Calamity did not appear until twenty-five years after her death. Once those images crystallized in the 1920s and 1930s, one indisputable conclusion became clear: the legendary Calamity Jane, the lively heroine of the Old West, would always attract more attention and interest than the Martha Jane Canary of history.

Even before she turned twenty-one, Martha Jane Canary was transformed into Calamity Jane.[1] Who supplied the name is not clear. It may have been any one of the railroaders, soldiers, or scouts and bullwackers, who had consorted with her before she was out of her teens. But Calamity Jane she had become before she rode into booming Deadwood in midsummer 1876. Already known as an independent-minded, free-spirited female who dressed, rode, and drove teams like a man, Calamity had emerged as a notorious figure, a rousing drinker, and perhaps a part-time prostitute.

Within the next two years, Calamity blossomed as a dime novel heroine, which greatly expanded her new reputation as a lively figure of the Wild West. When dime novelist Edward L. Wheeler casts Calamity as a protagonist in his *Deadwood Dick, the Prince of the Road; or, The Black Rider of the Black Hills* (1877) and in *Deadwood Dick on Deck; or, Calamity Jane, The Heroine of Whoop-Up* (1878), he betrays little acquaintance with her life. Instead he uses Calamity merely as another of a series of female frontier wildcats that include "Hurricane Nell," "Rowdy Kate," "Wild Edna," or "Phantom Moll." Wheeler distorts Calamity's biography,

---

[1] Two census reports—those contained in the 1860 United States Census for Mercer County, Missouri, and the special 1869 territorial census for Piedmont, Carter County, Wyoming—are exceptionally persuasive evidence for accepting 1856, Princeton, Missouri, as Martha Jane Canary's birth date and birth place. Unfortunately, the 1869 Wyoming census gives the age of "Martha Canary" as 15, not 13. Calamity probably added two years to her age because her lifestyle badly bruised society's expectations for a new teenager. No biographer has cited both of these census reports.

This romanticized depiction of Calamity Jane bore the title, "Miss Martha Canary ('Calamity Jane'), the female scout," in *The Coming Empire* (1878), by H. N. Maguire. (Montana Historical Society Library)

yet his bittersweet depiction of her in *Deadwood Dick on Deck* as a boisterous, cigar-smoking, wild-riding young woman, still attractive, with "a breast of alabaster purity," parallels the ambiguous reputation Calamity had already gained in western railroad camps and boomtowns.[2] This oxymoronic figure also dominates the pages of Mrs. William Loring Spencer's novel *Calamity Jane, A Story of the Black Hills* (1887).[3] Here, too, Calamity stands out in her first appearance, when she invades a picnic gathering of well-to-do women. As one character muses, "She had heard of Calamity Jane whose eccentricities were so numerous and daring, so remarkable, that she was suspected to be in every deviltry from robbing trains to playing faro."[4] Although the society ladies treat Calamity as a gate-crashing leper, the author also salutes her devotion to the sick and her protection of the beautiful, naive heroine. These conflicting images— Calamity as a buckskin-clad tippler and sexually promiscuous woman versus the sympathetic nurse and protector of the sick and downtrodden—appeared early in fictional and historical depictions and remain, more than a century later, the chief tension of her legend.

Calamity likewise added to her legend-in-the-making. In the mid-1890s, probably as a result of an invitation to appear as a featured attraction with a traveling show, Calamity supposedly wrote, but more likely dictated, her autobiography. Published as *Life and Adventures of Calamity Jane*, the book emphasizes her life up to the early 1880s (as do nearly all popular accounts).[5] Calamity falsely claims to have been a scout with several major military undertakings in the northern West. Of her clashes with the law, her numerous difficulties with a series of lovers and "husbands,"

---

[2] Calamity appeared as the heroine in several other dime novels, perhaps as many as ten, most written by Edward Wheeler.

[3] (Mrs.) William Loring Spencer, *Calamity Jane, A Story of the Black Hills* (New York: Cassell and Company, 1887).

[4] Ibid., 77.

[5] *Life and Adventures of Calamity Jane by Herself* (Np.: np., [1896?])

and her battles with alcoholism she makes no mention. Less than a decade later, upon her death in August 1903, an obituary in the New York *Times*, based primarily on her unreliable autobiography, described her as "the most eccentric and picturesque woman in the West" and credited her with having "participated in some of the most thrilling incidents of the then Wild West." The headline for the story was even more emotionally charged—and inaccurate. Calamity, the paper said, was the "Woman Who Became Famous as an Indian Fighter /. . . [The] Most Picturesque Character in the West."[6] In death, as in life, Calamity Jane became a charter member of the Wild West pantheon.

Interestingly, the legendary Calamity, so notorious in the generation before her death, largely disappeared from the scene in the next two decades, only to surface again in the 1920s. At much the same time that Walter Noble Burns and Stuart Lake turned out dramatic, journalistic biographies of such Wild West heroes as Billy the Kid and Wyatt Earp, that film Westerns dominated box offices throughout the country, and that the western novels of Zane Grey and Max Brand sold in the hundreds of thousands, newspaperman Duncan Aikman produced the first extensive account of Calamity's life. Similar to the biographies by Burns and Lake, Aikman's *Calamity Jane and the Lady Wildcats* (1927), which included a 130-page section on Calamity and chapters on Cattle Kate, Belle Starr, Lola Montez, and several others, overflowed with sensational details, contrived characterizations, and invented dialogues. Even more significant, Aikman's Calamity also resembles her sisters who appeared in fiction, films, and biographies from the 1920s through the 1950s. Stressing lively details, depicting Calamity as "one of the boys," and placing extraordinary emphasis on her early life, Aikman imitated previous creations of Calamity as a Wild West protagonist who lacked feminine manners or womanly appeal. Yet he also furnished the

---

[6] New York *Times*, August 2, 1903.

fullest account of her girlhood in Princeton, Missouri, largely based on interviews with a handful of residents who dimly remembered the Canary family from sixty years earlier. These vague remembrances of Calamity's vivacious but crude mother (rumored to have been rescued by marriage from a house of prostitution) and her dreamy, inefffectual father remain the most extensive discussion of her parents any biographer has provided.[7]

One suspects, however, that two films, one released in the 1930s and the other in the 1950s, did even more to shape the dominant romantic image of Calamity between World War I and the 1960s. In *The Plainsman* (1936), against a backdrop of western conflict and settlement from Abraham Lincoln's death in 1865 to Wild Bill Hickok's assassination eleven years later, director Cecil B. DeMille spectacularly dramatizes the love story of Wild Bill and Calamity. The romance of Wild Bill (Gary Cooper) and Calamity (Jean Arthur) rapidly unfolds before a wide-stage setting of battles with Indians, General George Armstrong Custer's defeat, and the drama of making the West safe for settlers.

Similar to Doris Day in *Calamity Jane* (1953), Arthur's Calamity is spunky, perky, and pretty, able to tend bar, drive a stage, and deftly handle a whip. She also loves Bill, throwing herself at him a half-dozen times. But Hickok fails to respond, even though admitting on one occasion that he loves her. Just before he is murdered, Bill tells Calamity that the West is rapidly changing and that he, like Buffalo Bill, may settle down. When he speaks of this possible transformation, Calamity reminds him about needing a home and someone to tend it, all but nominating herself for the task.

One scene from *The Plainsman* is especially heavy with symbolic intent and encapsulates DeMille's interpretation of Calamity. Preparing to ride for help for soldiers pinned down by Indians, Calamity steps out of the nearly destroyed

[7] Duncan Aikman, *Calamity Jane and the Lady Wildcats* (New York: H. Holt and Company, 1927).

skirt of a stylish dress she had donned earlier, hoping to prove her femininity, and rides for reinforcements in the buckskins worn beneath her dress. Moving back and forth from dress to leather pants, she personifies the oxymoronic legend of Calamity that had crystallized by the 1930s. Assertive and courageous (but not sexy or loose), DeMille's Calamity plays a vernacular woman of the frontier who wishes to marry. In allowing Bill's death, not hers, to close the film, however, the director undercuts her centrality to the movie's plot.

Although a few critics argue that Jean Arthur (remembered primarily as the wife and mother in *Shane*) was miscast as Calamity in *The Plainsmen*, most think Doris Day was ideally suited for the heroine of the musical Western *Calamity Jane*. Pretty, agile, and unable to disguise her attractive figure even under bulky buckskins, Day epitomizes in every way the romantic Wild West heroine. Her role in *Calamity Jane* as a lively, vivacious frontier woman fits smoothly into the well-known tradition of Annie Oakley in *Annie Get Your Gun* (1950).

The movie clearly achieves what it sets out to accomplish. An appealing mix of romance, adventure, and frenetic action, *Calamity Jane* uses only the most superficial biographical and historical facts. It avoids mentioning that Wild Bill was killed less than two months after he arrived in Deadwood in 1876 and that there is nothing in the historical record to indicate he and Calamity were together during those short weeks. Nor is there any indication here of Calamity's excessive drinking and possible prostitution. Instead, the movie depicts her as an innocent of the Wild West with a warm "female" heart, bursting with sentiment, humor, good-old-boyism, and, if necessary, jealousy.

One might argue, of course, that nothing more should be expected of a musical in the 1950s. True enough, but other film directors, novelists, and popularizers were following this romantic Calamity as well. In fact, prior to the dramatic sociocultural shifts of the 1960s and early 1970s, most Americans, whether fictionists, moviemakers, historians, readers, or members of other audiences, seemed to prefer a Wild West heroine like that starring in *Calamity Jane*.[8] Perhaps the widespread attachment to this idealistic type was the major impetus for the new kinds of Calamities who invaded and dominated novels and films after the 1960s.

Revealingly, the 1950s, a decade in which Westerns monopolized television and Hollywood and when a popular Kansas president—Dwight D. Eisenhower—inhabited the White House and paraded his western background, also spawn-ed three book-length biographies of Calamity Jane: Glenn Clairmonte's *Calamity Was the Name for Jane* (1959), Nolie Mumey's *Calamity Jane* (1950), and Roberta Beed Sollid's *Calamity Jane: A Study in Historical Criticism* (1958). Less romantic and more factually accurate than contemporary films and fiction focusing on Calamity, Mumey's and Sollid's biographies, even after forty years, remain among the most extensive of her lifestories.

Of the three, Clairmonte's *Calamity Was the Name for Jane* is the least successful because it is novelized biography rather than footnoted history. The volume contains too many imagined conversations and recreated scenes to be a dependable source on Calamity's life. One should not dismiss it, nonetheless, as the worst biography ever written, as one scholar did, because the author makes good use of clippings files and produces a smoothly written biographical novel based on Calamity's life.[9]

---

[8] Other films from the 1920s through the 1950s featuring major Calamity Jane characters were: *Wild Bill Hickok* (1923—Ethel Grey Terry); *The Paleface* (1948—Jane Russell); and *Calamity Jane and Sam Bass* (1959—Yvonne De Carlo). The only Calamity novel of note during this period was Ethel Hueston, *Calamity Jane of Deadwood Gulch* (Indianapolis: Bobbs-Merrill Company, 1937).

[9] Glenn Clairmonte, *Calamity Was the Name for Jane* (Denver: Sage Books, 1959). Leonard Jennewein to Agnes Wright Spring, December 28, 1959, box 25, Agnes Wright Spring Papers, American Heritage Center, Laramie, Wyoming. For a balanced evaluation, see Roberta Beed Sollid, review of *Calamity Was the Name* in *Montana The Magazine of Western History*, 10 (July 1960), 70.

Author H. N. Maguire took the photograph that served as the original for this illustration in his book, *The Coming Empire* (1878). Friends "Arapahoe Joe" and "Colorado Charley" provided the epitaph "Pard, we will meet again in the happy hunting grounds, to part no more" (p. 63). (Montana Historical Society Library)

The briefest of the three biographies, Mumey's uncritical *Calamity Jane* is based largely on the author's periodical research. Unfortunately, however, the volume is little more than a narrative compilation of these news stories rather than a careful weighing of the conflicting facts and opinions about Calamity.[10] A medical doctor, a dedicated local historian, and an author of several privately printed volumes, Mumey accepts without much reservation the most controversial source about Calamity: her alleged letters and diary addressed to "Janie" (Jean Hickok McCormick), who claimed to be the daughter of Calamity and Wild Bill Hickok and who announced the existence of the manuscripts in the 1940s.[11] Mumey devotes almost one-third of his 140-page biography to the first full publication of this largely discredited source, but he seems not to have subjected the letters and diary to the most widely accepted methods of testing documents for their historical authenticity.

The third and best of the trilogy of biographies, Sollid's *Calamity Jane*, is the most useful lifestory yet published. Based almost entirely on Sollid's master's thesis completed at the University of Montana in 1951, Sollid's book clearly illustrates her diligent research and her practical approach to historical writing. With a degree in psychology from Stanford and service in the United States Navy during World War II, Sollid arrived in Montana in the late 1940s and soon decided to learn the history of her adopted region. Under the steady encouragement of noted western historian Paul C. Phillips, Sollid set out to write a thesis on Calamity Jane

---

[10]Nolie Mumey, *Calamity Jane, 1852–1903: A History of Her Life and Adventures in the West* (Denver: Range Press, 1950). Interview with Norma Flynn Mumey, September 5, 1994.

[11]Several condensed versions of the alleged diary and letters have been published as *Calamity Jane's Diary and Letters* ([Billings, Mont.]: Don C. and Stella A. Foote, 1951 and after). For thorough and strong evidence against accepting the diary and letters as Calamity's, see revealing material collected in the Clarence Paine Papers, Center for Western Studies, Augustana College, Sioux Falls, South Dakota. A useful exercise would be to study the diary and letters as an attempt by a later party to fathom what Calamity might have thought privately had she written to a daughter about her life.

but soon ran into difficulty with historical sources. Failing to locate reliable material on which to base her project, she embarked on an extended bus trip to visit numerous libraries and archives and to copy every pertinent document, all laboriously typed in those pre-xerox days.[12]

Sollid's book is not so much a biography as a thorough thematic discussion of all the facts then available on Calamity. Nor will the reader find a clear thesis running throughout the text. Rather, the author succinctly states her problem—"no career is so elusive to the historian as that of a loose woman"—and then attempts to summarize the major stories about Calamity, emphasizing those that seem most reliable.[13] As well-known western historian Robert Riegel pointed out, romanticists could be unhappy with Sollid because she not only torpedoed numerous misleading tales, she provided a valuable analytical discussion of a notable Wild West character seldom subjected to such exacting scrutiny. Those who "desire[d] to know the truth about Calamity Jane," Riegel added, would find her book "fascinating."[14] Although Sollid obviously had not set out to pummel previous writers as irresponsible sensationalists, her matter-of-fact treatment of Calamity provided a painstakingly researched lifestory that had eluded most earlier biographers.

The decade stretching from President John Kennedy's death in 1963 to the mid-1970s, in which so many facets of American society and culture experienced the buffeting blows of stress and change, was also a watershed period for interpretations of the American West. Sometimes during those dozen years but particularly afterwards, traditional interpretations of the heroic Euro-American settling of the West

---

[12]Roberta Beed Sollid, *Calamity Jane: A Study in Historical Criticism* (Helena, Mont.: Western Press, 1958). Interview with Roberta B. Sollid, September 2, 1994.

[13]Sollid, *Calamity Jane*, xi.

[14]Robert E. Riegel, review of *Calamity Jane: A Study in Historical Criticism* in *Montana The Magazine of Western History*, 9 (January 1959), 63.

underwent dramatic transformations. In such movies as *Little Big Man* (1970), *The Wild Bunch* (1969), and the "dollars" films starring Clint Eastwood, in dozens of histories and biographies exemplifying a new western historiography stressing race, gender, and environmental topics, and in novels such as Robert Flynn's *North to Yesterday* (1967), David Wagoner's *Where Is My Wandering Boy Tonight?* (1970), and John Seelye's *The Kid* (1972), images of an optimistic, romantic Wild West were challenged, reoriented, or destroyed. Not surprisingly, at the same time, less optimistic images of Calamity Jane replaced those popular before the 1960s.

If the two movies *The Plainsman* and *Calamity Jane* greatly influenced the formation of the romantic legend of Calamity, two novels, Pete Dexter's *Deadwood* (1986) and Larry McMurtry's *Buffalo Girls* (1990), helped to engender a new gray Calamity for the generation after 1970.[15] No one would mistake the heroine of *Deadwood* for any of the earlier Calamities. Not much cleaner than the filthy tents and lean-tos into which she flops, Dexter's Calamity smells like the ripe mules and horses she rides. Unwashed, unloved, and under-appreciated, she seems less a woman than a two-legged screaming eagle bent on shooting off toes, bragging of her "husband" Wild Bill, and out-drinking all others, men and vile drunkards included. Calamity is so rancid that a fresh crop of mold grows unnoticed on her neck, and no man pays much attention to her even though fornication and sexual violence rule in Dexter's Deadwood. Only when a vicious epidemic of smallpox invades the boomtown does Calamity serve a purpose: God made her, she and the author imply, to minister to the sick.

Unfortunately, the Calamity of *Deadwood* is unbelievable—perhaps as much from the limits of parody as from the weaknesses of the novel and its heroine. Nearly all the author's characters, Calamity included, are ludicrous, hy-

---

[15]Pete Dexter, *Deadwood* (New York: Random House, 1986); Larry McMurtry, *Buffalo Girls: A Novel* (New York: Simon and Schuster, 1990).

perbolic caricatures. These excesses lead to a simply stated problem: once the earlier, too-simplistic, and romantic legends about Calamity, Wild Bill, and their supporting cast have been roundly lampooned through satire and parody, what remains in the novel? Not much. The abundant energy, humor, and attractiveness of *Deadwood*, once lavishly expended in countering Wild West stereotypes, leave too little for memorable characterizations or probing cultural comment. In this regard, one must admit that we lack memorable western novels whose central purposes are to correct earlier romantic stereotypes and yet retain sufficient literary power to be remembered for their artistic excellence. Perhaps Walter Van Tilburg Clark's *The Ox-Bow Incident* (1940) and several of H. L. Davis's superb novels come closest to these dual achievements, but they, too, fall short in comparison with the strongest western fiction of Willa Cather, John Steinbeck, and Wallace Stegner.[16]

Larry McMurtry's Calamity in *Buffalo Girls* also typifies an equivocal attitude toward the Old West. Aging, increasingly out of step with change, and unable to find new moorings, Calamity symbolizes here a closing frontier, a once-heroic past disappearing into nostalgic haze. Throughout, decline, despair, and death exude from McMurtry's novel.

McMurtry's Calamity comes on stage trying to understand how her West not only has vanished but is now being embalmed in Buffalo Bill's phoney Wild West show. Like her old mountain men friends Jim and Bartle, who search for the last beaver in the West, like the elderly Native American No Ears, and like her best friend Dora DuFran, madam and frustrated lover, Calamity is forced to exist in a West of memory. By the end of the novel we also realize that she has imagined a daughter to whom she writes her

[16]On H. L. Davis, see *Honey in the Horn* (1935) and *Winds of Morning* (1952). For examples of other work, see Willa Cather, *O Pioneers!* (1913), *My Antonia* (1918), and *Death Comes for the Archbishop* (1927); John Steinbeck, *Tortilla Flat* (1935), *The Grapes of Wrath* (1939), and *Cannery Row* (1945); and Wallace Stegner, *The Big Rock Candy Mountain* (1943) and *Angle of Repose* (1971).

tearful laments, and that she may have suffered from the frustrations of a hermaphroditic condition.

McMurtry depicts Calamity as a failure in nearly all of her endeavors. Unable to adjust to a closed frontier, she boozes and cries her way through much of the novel. She falls off the stagecoach in Buffalo Bill's Wild West, she is unable to use a gun (and thus unable to compete with Annie Oakley), and cannot *do* anything but live off others, especially Dora. McMurtry also implies how little space or acceptance existed in the Old West for a woman like Calamity, without husband, children, or calling. Although this novel also suffers from the excessive grayness and ambiguity that undermine Dexter's *Deadwood*, McMurtry raises significant cultural questions about the impact of a closing frontier and about the narrow, constricting roles forced on women in an imagined Wild West. He also moves beyond Dexter in not limiting his fiction to satirizing earlier cultural stereotypes.

Clearly, this new gray Calamity owes much to counter mythic images of several Wild West figures that emerged after the 1960s. The fictional and cinematic representations of George Custer in *Little Big Man* (novel in 1964, film in 1970), the filmic portraits of Billy the Kid in *Pat Garrett and Billy the Kid* (1973) and *Young Guns* (1988), and his bleak embodiment in McMurtry's novel *Anything for Billy* (1988), as well as the ambivalent points of view in Clint Eastwood's Oscar-winning film *Unforgiven* (1992), illustrate an ambiguous West that surfaced after the Kennedys and Camelot. But still other sociocultural shifts may produce a different kind of Calamity. Indeed, two recent essays, if taken as harbingers, suggest that a less ambivalent, neorealistic image may be coming into focus. Could it be that readers and viewers, now sufficiently aware of the excesses of romantic Calamities between the wars and of the antiheroines of the post-1960s, are receptive to a new shift in Calamity legend-making?

In a recent smoothly written essay, historian Elizabeth Stevenson indicates one direction in which a new realistic

Calamity might move.[17] Carefully studying the conflicting controversies surrounding Calamity, Stevenson produces a fact-filled, balanced overview, avoiding both the mawkish love stories of Calamity and Wild Bill as well as the black humor of recent novels. Another model for a neorealistic Calamity is that which history professor James McLaird supplies in his discussion of the last year of her life. Thoroughly researched and measured in tone, McLaird's biographical sketch reveals how much previous biographers of Calamity have overlooked, particularly in the dozens of stories that appeared monthly, even weekly, in newspapers across the northern interior West. The clear and abundant strengths of this brief essay promise that McLaird's nearly completed biography will be the definitive work on Calamity Jane.[18]

If these factual, even-handed essays by Stevenson and McLaird signal the emergence of a more realistic era of writing about Calamity, the pioneering biography by Roberta Beed Sollid takes on even greater significance. Published almost forty years ago and still the most thorough of the biographical studies of Calamity Jane, Sollid's book looms large as a pathbreaking volume owing more to the author's thorough research than to the unfortunate panderings of too many biographers, novelists, and filmmakers to Americans' unquenchable desire for Wild West romanticism. Perhaps the reprinting of her notable work will help spark a renewed interest in Calamity Jane as a redoubtable pioneer woman, and, in turn, to further examinations of a larger topic: the invention of an American Wild West. One hopes.

---

[17]Elizabeth Stevenson, "Who Was Calamity Jane? A Speculation," in *Figures in a Western Landscape: Men and Women of the Northern Rockies* (Baltimore: Johns Hopkins University Press, 1994), 146–72.

[18]James D. McLaird, "Calamity Jane: The Life and the Legend," *South Dakota History*, 24 (Spring 1994), 1–18.